The Siege of
LZ KATE

6/14/14

George Moesbeck:

Never underestimate the value of
artillerymen. That's one of the messages
in this book, which I am sure that
you learned in Korea.

Thanks for your service.

Cordially,
Art Sharp

The Siege of
LZ KATE

The Battle for an
American Firebase in Vietnam

Arthur G. Sharp

STACKPOLE
BOOKS

Published by
STACKPOLE BOOKS
5067 Ritter Road
Mechanicsburg, PA 17055
www.stackpolebooks.com

Printed in the United States of America

FIRST EDITION

10 9 8 7 6 5 4 3 2 1

Library of Congress Cataloging-in-Publication Data

Sharp, Arthur G.
  The siege of LZ Kate / by Arthur G. Sharp. — First edition.
      pages cm
  ISBN 978-0-8117-1386-3
1. Vietnam War, 1961–1975—Campaigns—Vietnam—Central Highlands. 2.
Military bases, American—Vietnam—History—20th century. 3. Central Highlands
(Vietnam)—History, Military—20th century. I. Title.
  DS557.8.C4S55 2014
  959.704'342—dc23
                                          2013051010

To the valorous American Vietnam veterans,
including two of my brothers, Terry and Duane,
who fought a war that was not popular at home but who
pulled together for one another, regardless of branch of service,
to enhance their chances of getting back safely to the World,
and especially to those who became unwitting victims
of Richard M. Nixon's Vietnamization policy.

Contents

Foreword: Why Firebase Kate? ix

Preface xi

Introduction xiii

Chapter 1   Let's Build Some Firebases 1

Chapter 2   Benhet 9

Chapter 3   Of All the Places in Victnam 22

Day 1: October 27, 1969 35

Chapter 4   Sergeant Pierelli Arrives 36

Day 2: October 28, 1969 39

Chapter 5   Captain Albracht Takes Command 40

Day 3: October 29, 1969 47

Chapter 6   *Crack! Boom!* 48

Chapter 7   The Captain Takes a Hit 58

Chapter 8   In a Fog 67

Day 4: October 30, 1969 75

Chapter 9   A "Black" Day for 48th AHC 76

Chapter 10 Tracers Can Be Traced 84

Day 5: October 31, 1969 91

Chapter 11   Trick or Treat 92
Chapter 12   The Cavalry Arrives 101
Chapter 13   Puff, the Magic Dragon 106
Chapter 14   A Dustoff and a Surprise 128
Chapter 15   Night Flight 133

Day 6: November 1, 1969 149

Chapter 16   D-Day 150
Chapter 17   Did I Miss Anything? 155
Chapter 18   E&E 162
Chapter 19   Confusion Reigns in the Skies 172
Chapter 20   Linkup 185
Chapter 21   Leaving Susan and Annie 193
Chapter 22   Mayhem and Medals 199
Chapter 23   Once upon a Time 207
Chapter 24   All for Naught? 214

Epilogue: Where Are They Now? 223
Acknowledgments 233

Foreword

Why Firebase Kate?

O f all the fire support bases and artillery raids in which I participated in Vietnam, the question was "Why Kate?" I think it came from a recurring nightmare that I had for years after returning from Vietnam.

In the 1970s, I saw the movie *Go Tell the Spartans*, a story about a small outpost in Vietnam that had to be abandoned by its Vietnamese contingent and American advisors. All but one American was lost. My dream always had the same beginning: my small contingent would be walking along when we would come upon a sign reading, "Welcome to Bon Sar Pa." The dream had several endings, but all were based on being overpowered by a huge force of NVA soldiers. I could never squeeze the trigger of my M16 hard enough for the rifle to fire as the force got closer and closer. When they were within feet of me, I would always wake up in a cold sweat. Awake, however, I could not remember anything about Bon Sar Pa; I don't know if it was forgotten or repressed.

Years later, in the mid-1990s, I began finally to sort through some of my memorabilia and found a notebook in which I had recorded some operations and dates. I also found a picture of a 105mm howitzer and crew on which I had written "Crew from LZ Kate." I knew Kate had something to do with my dream.

I began to recall more and also obtained material from archives and other sources. Then I remembered my interview with Colonel Anderson, the deputy commanding officer of IFFV (I Field Force Vietnam) Artillery, in 1969 when I went to meet Col. Charles Hall and interview to be a general's aide. Col. Anderson showed me the plan of the firebases around Duclap and Buprang, which was about 110 miles northwest of Saigon and within seven miles of the Cambodian border. (The Cambodian border was so close people could reach it by walking east, north, or west from Buprang.) We also talked about how he was going to name the firebases for his wife and daughters.

I began to remember the names of the other firebases and what had taken place. In my research I got a map, and there was Bon Sar Pa. I saw its proximity to Duclap and remembered the volcano. Everything was coming back. I remembered the frustration and confusion of losing all these firebases because there was an argument about whether it was an American or Vietnamese operation. Because no one could settle the debate, no one would act.

I remembered the fear and frustration when we found that we had a lack of aviation fuel, which delayed the evacuation of Firebases Susan and Annie. I especially remembered the total frustration and sorrow for the loss of Ron Ross on Kate and for the loss of James Gaiser, who was part of a relief convoy to the area several days later. I saw the sunken look in the faces of the 105mm howitzer crew as they were interviewed about Michael Robert Norton, the one soldier who did not survive the breakout from Kate. Even though I didn't know him, it left me with a sick feeling to think that we might never know what happened to him. I remembered the feeling of hopelessness when it seemed we could do nothing right to save these men and the firebases.

Then there was the anger as the Army of the Republic of Vietnam command arrogantly refused to take any action or responsibility. In any event, I began to research logs and reports looking for documentation of a Bronze Star I was told I would be getting before we took the 105mm howitzer crew back to Duc Trong. When I began to dig into the information about the firebases and recalled what happened at Kate, my selfish desires became an embarrassment in light of the desperate situation these men faced. When I discovered that William Albracht had received no recognition for what I considered a heroic effort in saving these artillerymen, I changed my attitude and decided their story had to be told.

Reginald Brockwell
Architect of Firebase Kate

Preface

On Friday, October 31, 1969, Led Zeppelin appeared at the Springfield, Massachusetts, Memorial Auditorium. The number one song at the time was Elvis Presley's "Suspicious Minds." That same day, Wal-Mart incorporated as Wal-Mart Stores Inc.; a race riot took place in Jacksonville, Florida; and Lenny Wilkens, the second-winningest coach in NBA history, earned his first victory when his Seattle SuperSonics defeated the Cincinnati Royals, 129 to 121. Life in the United States went on as usual on Halloween night in 1969, but as *Time* magazine reported in its October 31 issue, "Nearly five years after the 1965 buildup, Americans are increasingly impatient for a way out of Viet Nam, skeptical about the outcome of the fighting and ambivalent about the means of ending it."

Approximately 8,100 miles away from Springfield, Massachusetts, two young U.S. Army Special Forces soldiers, Capt. William Albracht and Sgt. Daniel Pierelli, were, like their fellow Americans back home, seeking a way out of Vietnam. But first they had to figure out a way to save 150 U.S. artillerymen and Montagnard security forces whose lives were in their hands. The troops were at a firebase named Kate, which was surrounded by approximately 5,000 North Vietnam Army (NVA) soldiers intent on killing them and destroying the base. The defenders at Kate were not concerned about getting tickets to a sold-out Led Zeppelin concert or whether Lenny Wilkens was beginning his path to glory. All they wanted to do was punch their tickets home. They did, eventually, but not all of them made the trip.

As Led Zeppelin followed up its Springfield concert with another the next night in Syracuse, New York, Albracht and Pierelli led their

band of warriors to safety through a torrent of enemy and friendly bullets, mortar rounds, and artillery shells. Their escape did not get most
of them any closer to home, though. They stayed in Vietnam, finished
their tours, and remained silent about their experiences at Kate. They
were, after all, soldiers, and that is what soldiers do. Their story went
largely unnoticed—until now.

This account of their harrowing escape and evasion from Kate
makes rock concerts, hit songs, and basketball games seem inconse-
quential by comparison.

Introduction

*"No event in American history is more misunderstood
than the Vietnam War. It was misreported then,
and it is misremembered now."*

—RICHARD M. NIXON, 1985

As the United States' participation in the Vietnam War continued in its fifth year in 1969, enemy troops appeared to be growing more active in the area of Nhon Co, Buprang, and Duclap in the Central Highlands near the Cambodian border. The North Vietnamese Army (NVA) had besieged Duclap during the fall of 1968 and been beaten back. There was abundant intelligence that they would be attacking again in the fall of 1969.

Since the "friendlies"—as Americans, Australians, South Koreans, South Vietnamese, and other allied forces will be known throughout this book—knew the NVA was coming, commanders established several remote firebases, named Kate, Helen, Dory, Susan, and Annie, around Buprang, from which their artillery could help defend the main camp. Not surprisingly, the NVA attacked the remote firebases first, rather than Buprang, since the bases were close to its camps in Cambodia and infiltration routes into Vietnam. Helen, one of the smaller firebases, was the first to be evacuated. That happened on October 29 when it came under attack by multiple NVA battalions. The others would fall or be evacuated one by one at later dates. Dorrie was less susceptible to the NVA because it was larger than the other firebases and was intended to be a permanent facility.

Attacking smaller bases and outposts was standard practice for the NVA. They employed this strategy to lure friendly forces into ambushes or divert them from operations elsewhere. Thus, the remote jungle outpost known as Kate became a small part of the NVA's fall 1969 campaign against the Special Forces camps near Buprang and Duclap.

The battle for Kate may have been small in terms of the overall war, but it was immense as far as the 30 U.S. Army artillerymen, 120 Montagnard security forces, and scores of helicopter and other aircraft pilots defending the base were concerned. A considerable number of U.S. aircraft were involved in the battle for Kate and the other firebases. Their losses were significant. Among them, the 7/17th Cavalry lost three helicopters shot down in a flak trap near Buprang, resulting in one pilot killed in action, one pilot rescued, and four pilots and crew members captured, although two of them were released within a couple of weeks. (A flak trap is a tactic in which a military unit places multiple weapons such as machine guns and missiles along a route used by helicopters and fires them in a coordinated matter.) Two pilots were sent to the infamous Vietnamese prison known as the Hanoi Hilton, and at least one came home as part of a POW release. Other helicopter units that suffered losses included the 48th Assault Helicopter Company (AHC), which lost one gunship that was shot down near Kate with the deaths of all four crew members; the 281st Assault Helicopter Company, from which one gunship was shot down at Volcano, near Duclap, with no loss of life (all four crew members were rescued); the 155th Assault Helicopter Company, from which one pilot was wounded at Buprang and two pilots were wounded at Volcano; and the 559th Tactical Fighter Squadron, USAF, which lost an F-4C jet interceptor fighter/fighter-bomber and two pilots killed in action near Buprang on December 1, 1969.

The losses contradicted a November 1969 *Time* magazine article that reported Vietnamese helicopters were doing most of the flying at Buprang and Duclap. U.S. pilots laughed at the report. One, Les Davison, wrote a letter to the magazine, telling them they didn't have their facts straight. A magazine correspondent replied that Davison didn't know what he was talking about.

The facts of the battle supported Davison's view. But the facts about the war in Vietnam have long been withheld from the public's knowledge, as U.S. Army Special Forces Captain William Albracht, one of the key players in the story of Kate, noted years after the battle ended. Albracht led his troops to safety in the face of certain death or capture by a determined and vastly larger enemy force—and did so while ignoring his own safety during six of the deadliest days that any soldier could ever endure. What makes his accomplishments at Kate even more remarkable was that at the time he was the youngest captain in the Special Forces at age twenty-one. His maturity and leadership skills belied his age.

Kate was a microbattle in the macrowar. It was a classic example of what happened when political meddling interfered with the conduct of the war in Vietnam. That is why, Albracht explained, "It is great story that needs to be told. It has a beginning, middle, and a good ending."

The lead-up to Kate began early in 1969, when the NVA attacked firebases around Benhet, a South Vietnamese outpost near Cambodia that was the focus of a fifty-five-day siege in June and July. Even though friendly forces drove the NVA off eventually, their commanders knew the battle for the region was far from over. They anticipated another NVA push later that year on numerous Special Forces camps around Buprang and Duclap. With that in mind, Headquarters, U.S. Army Vietnam (HQ USARV) decided in August 1969 to counteract the possible threat and turned operational control of these camps over to the 23rd Division of the Army of the Republic of Vietnam (ARVN). Fire support bases were to be established to support Mobile Strike Force (MSF) reconnaissance-in-force operations, including three bases in the Buprang tactical area of responsibility: Annie, Susan, and Kate.

Detachment B-23, Company B, of the 5th Special Forces Group (Airborne), was assigned to provide camp strike force units as security elements for the fire support bases on a periodic basis. B-23 was also directed to provide the firebases with a captain or major as a commander. It became the responsibility of the 5th Battalion, 22nd Artillery, to provide the artillery for the bases. The 155th AHC, based at Ban Me Thuot, one of the largest cities in the region, provided helicopter support, including medevacs (Dustoffs), cranes (CH-47s), troop and supply carriers (slicks), and gunships to protect the others. Daring pilots flew a variety of missions, ranging from recon ("sniffers") to taxi services. The 155th played a central role in the siege of and escape from Kate and the support of other firebases and camps in the area. Captain Anthony Giordano, the 155th's operations officer during most of 1969, noted that additional assets were based out of Ban Me Thout during the operations in late 1969, which suggested an increased level of concern on the high command's part regarding the NVA's threat to the region and the allies' ability to defeat it.

At the outset, enemy activity around the firebases was almost non-existent. It was if the NVA were ignoring them. Perhaps because of the weather—the summer monsoon season ran from June through September—the NVA waited until late October to act against the bases. Likewise, friendly forces did not make any great effort during the monsoon season to locate the NVA. Wind and rain made it difficult for chopper pilots to fly sniffer missions, and the bad weather limited ground activities. The MSF elements of Company B operating in the Buprang tactical area of responsibility sent out occasional recon patrols, but they did not make any significant contact with enemy forces. That did not mean the NVA were not there. In fact, they were.

Allied Special Agent Reports indicated that NVA battalion- and regiment-size elements were moving in and around the Buprang area to the north and northwest of the camp there. Other Special Agent Reports revealed that several enemy units were located in Cambodia, right across the border. Yet contact between friendly and NVA troops was extremely limited.

Once NVA elements were located, the 7/17 Cavalry continually sent out helicopter patrols in the areas where they had been spotted. Suddenly, in late October, the patrols noticed that the NVA was on the move. 7/17 Cavalry elements started tracking a large NVA troop concentration at a base camp in Cambodia. The enemy's regimental command post began a rapid deployment from the northwest to the north, then to the northeast of Camp Buprang. And the NVA troops kept moving. One NVA regimental command post appeared headed for Kate. During the ensuing battle, the command post moved to approximately one and a half miles southeast of Kate, then relocated approximately two miles south of it. The NVA was hard to pin down.

Once the NVA made its presence known, however, it was game on. Kate bore the brunt of the assaults for six days, until two Special Forces soldiers, a courageous captain and a standout sergeant, led approximately 150 troops under their command to safety during one of the most daring escape-and-evasion operations of the Vietnam War. The story of their daring, traumatic escape from Kate and linkup with an MSF, or "Mike Force" unit after a three-klick (one klick equals one kilometer), five-hour odyssey is the subject of this book.

Chapter 1

Let's Build Some Firebases

"The defense of freedom is everybody's business, not just America's business. And it is particularly the responsibility of the people whose freedom is threatened. In the previous administration, we Americanized the war in Vietnam. In this administration, we are Vietnamizing the search for peace."

—RICHARD M. NIXON, NOVEMBER 3, 1969

Thank You, Mr. Nixon

There has been a recent trend in American politics toward *ization* policies as a way of backing away from a war. It began in Vietnam and continues to this day.

Here is how the policy works. The government gets involved in a war with good intentions (although "good" is debatable). Then, once officials realize that the war is dragging on with no end in sight, growing more expensive than originally planned, and becoming increasingly unpopular among the public, they seek a way out. The preferred method of extrication when the tipping point is reached is to turn responsibility for the war gradually over to the government it originally sought to help. Often, the American administration is not the one that initiated the military operation. There is at least one major drawback to the policy: it puts U.S. troops at increased risk as the withdrawal progresses. That was the case in Vietnam.

The Vietnamization plan was launched following Secretary of Defense Melvin R. Laird's visit to Vietnam in March 1969. Under the plan, President Nixon ordered a substantial increase in the training and equipment of South Vietnamese forces. Nixon explained his Vietnamization policy to the American people in a speech to the nation on November 3, 1969. By that time, the troops at Kate had experienced what it meant to them at the local level—and it almost cost them their lives.

Meanwhile, the American troops in-country were susceptible to sometimes capricious decisions made by ARVN officials that put them in compromised positions. That is what happened to the approximately 30 U.S. troops of diverse backgrounds and 120 Montagnard mercenaries assigned to Kate in the northeastern part of South Vietnam, near the Cambodian border, about six miles east-southeast of Special Forces Camp A-236 at Buprang and two miles west-southwest of the Cambodian border.

The COSVN Reaction

Nixon's Vietnamization policy did not go unnoticed by enemy administrators and government leaders, who reacted strongly to minimize it. They had their own political structure in place, called COSVN (Central Office for South Vietnam), to govern the region. The Lao Dong Central Executive Committee originally established COSVN in 1951 to command the insurgency in southern Vietnam during the first Indochina War. It was dissolved after the 1954 Geneva cease-fire agreement but was reactivated in 1961 to direct all communist military and political activities in South Vietnam. As such, COSVN controlled the People's Revolutionary Party, the National Liberation Front, and the Viet Cong.

COSVN emphasized pursuit of extended warfare that would lead to a political victory. The plan was revealed in a document titled *COSVN Resolution 9*, which was captured during an ambush on October 9, 1969, by members of the 199th Light Infantry Brigade. North

Vietnamese leaders believed that if they halted the allied pacification program and inflicted heavy losses on the friendly forces—or "puppets," as they were fond of calling the enemy—they could achieve victory, albeit a limited one. That, in turn, would increase antiwar sentiment in the United States. As a result, they postulated, Nixon would have to withdraw at least some, if not all, of the American forces in South Vietnam and accept a coalition government. Without U.S. military aid, the Republic of Vietnam would be unable to achieve a military victory over the North. It, too, would have to participate in the proposed coalition government. Gradually, according to the COSVN plan, the communists would assume control of that government.

Before any of that could happen, however, the NVA had to win some decisive victories in the Mekong Delta, in the jungle, and in the mountains. Enter Kate.

Giving Birth to Kate

Headquarters, U.S. Army Republic of Vietnam (HQ USARV) decided in August 1969 that establishing fire support bases (FSBs), or simply firebases, in the northwestern areas of Nhon Co, Buprang, and Duclap would be wise. There existed the possibility of enemy activity in the area, which could pose a threat to Special Forces A Camps, and there were signs that the NVA would move in and out of nearby Cambodia to conduct attacks on allied troops and facilities. The firebases were created to prevent or forestall those attacks and support Mobile Strike Force reconnaissance-in-force operations in the vicinity. Camp Strike Force elements would be assigned to provide local security and defend the firebases.

According to Col. Francis Bowers, commander of the Provisional Artillery Group, headquarters for all American artillery batteries in the southern II Corps region, "These firebases were never designed to be permanent locations." As it turned out, he was right—but for the wrong reasons. Furthermore, HQ USARV decided that operational control of the camps and the firebases should be turned over to the

23rd ARVN Division in a bow to "Vietnamization." This also turned out to be a bad idea for the defenders of Landing Zone (LZ) Kate.

In September, the U.S. Army set up three firebases in the Buprang Tactical Area of Responsibility: Annie, Susan, and Kate, named for the daughters of Col. Charles Hall, commanding officer of the I Field Force Vietnam Artillery, whose promotion to general was imminent. The bases were separate, but mutually supportive of one another.

Francis Barnes, a member of First Field Forces, C Battery, 1/92 Artillery, explained the relationships between and among the bases: "Our home base was Pleiku artillery hill in the Central Highlands. Then, in September 1969, our battery was split up. Two 155mm towed artillery guns were airlifted to Kate, and two were airlifted to Susan." He did not remember what happened to the battery's other two guns. "There was a bit of irony in the gun designations. Even though they were officially 155mm towed guns, there was no way to tow them around Kate or the other firebases. What roads existed in the area were unsuitable for transporting guns, troops, materiel . . . anything that was needed on the bases."

The Mission Changes

The firebases were located on hilltops, and the NVA had control of the roads. Therefore, supplies and personnel were transported by helicopters, which were protected by a variety of fighter-bombers, observation planes, and heavily armed gunships known as Spooky (U.S. Air Force AC-47) and Shadow (U.S. Air Force AC-119). The pilots put their lives at risk every day. It is possible that without their efforts, the entire complement of Kate would have died before they escaped, and the troops on the other firebases might have as well.

Barnes landed on Susan two days before his twenty-first birthday. His battery commander, Capt. Klaus M. Adam, let him celebrate on the base, but there was precious little time for a party. There was work to do, even though the base was relatively quiet at that point. "Our mission on Susan was like all missions," Barnes said. "Support the infantry. On this mission, we had Montagnards and some of the 25th, if my memory serves me correctly." But their assignment soon changed. "Our Top [sergeant] came to us to inform us that our two guns and others were in jeopardy of being overrun on Kate. He stressed that we needed to put extra fire out in support of Kate and their mission."

The troops on Susan could not concern themselves totally with Kate. Elements of the NVA regulars were prodding them to draw support away from Kate. Susan, Kate, Buprang, Du Loc, Annie—it did not make a difference. They were all tied inextricably together. The survival of one depended on mutual assistance from the others. The army brass recognized that. They chose the best troops available to operate and protect the firebases.

The responsibility for providing camp strike force units was assigned to Detachment A-236, Company B, 5th SFGA, whose executive officer was Capt. William Albracht. The army needed experienced officers as commanders and assigned captains or majors to these positions. The detachment selected the personnel from its subordinate A Camps as security elements for the fire support bases on a periodic basis. Of course, firebases needed artillery units. These came from the 5th Battalion, 22nd Artillery (U.S.).

Everything was in place. Early on, the army personnel assigned to the firebases had to wonder if their presence was needed in the area.

What Enemy Activity?

There was no indication at first that the enemy had any interest in attacking the firebases or even acknowledging their existence. Mobile Strike Force elements of Company B operating in the area did not make any sizable contacts with enemy forces between September and late October. Special Agent Reports indicated that enemy battalion- and regiment-size headquarters were moving in and around Buprang's tactical area of responsibility to the north and northwest of the camp, and agents indicated that several enemy units were located in Cambodia. But they were not near the firebases until late October. That was reflected in the 155th Commander's Monthly Highlights for October 1969:

1. <u>OPERATIONS</u>

a. October marked the end of the rainy season for the Central Highlands. With the good weather the company's flying statistics increased measurably and a total of 2815 hours of flight time accrued. During this period the 155th continued to provide aviation support for the 23rd ARVN Division, Detachment B-236 (5th Special Forces Group), and units within Darlac, Quang Duc, and Tuyen Duc Provinces.

The primary mission of the company continued to be support of B-50 operations which, during October, were staged out of Duc Co. Sniffer missions in support of G-2, 23rd ARVN Division and B-236 were conducted daily in southern Darlac and throughout all of Quang Duc, concentrating on Buprang, Ghia Nia, and Duclap.

b. October also marked the beginning of the long awaited Communist offensive in the Buprang, Ghia Nia, Duclap Triangle. Large size enemy units moved into the areas south of Buprang and into areas southwest of Duclap. The 155th provided immediate support to units threatened by these forces. It provided MEDEVAC aircraft to assist units under siege at the 5/22nd Artillery firebases south of Buprang and Duclap. It provided aircraft to resupply Kate, which came under sustained attack on 31 October.

On many occasions 155 aircraft carried much needed ammunition, food, and water to Kate while in danger of constant and heavy enemy fire. This resupply effort to Kate was culminated by an emergency night resupply of ammunition to Kate during the early morning hours of 1 November 1969. Five slicks and four gunships of the 155th lifted 4000 pounds of the much needed supplies into Kate without incident.

The story did not sound very exciting on paper. Off paper, for the troops on the ground, it was a much different tale.

In late October, troops from the 7/17 Cavalry patrolling the northwestern portion of the Buprang tactical area of responsibility found only small reconnaissance enemy activity. The same held true for the western section. 7/17 troops reported two items of interest: Confirmed intelligence reports cited large concentrations of enemy units northwest of Buprang. They also located a large enemy base camp in Cambodia, right across the border. Suddenly, enemy troops were on the move.

Special Agent Reports indicated that the enemy regimental command posts initiated a rapid deployment from the northwest to the north and then to the northeast of Camp Buprang. At the same time, the regimental command post relocated to within thirteen miles of Kate—and then moved again to a position only 1.8 miles away. Their movements bore watching.

The enemy troops that eventually attacked Kate were identified as elements of the 28th and 66th NVA Heavy Infantry Regiments, the 40th NVA Artillery Regiment, and the K394 Artillery Battalion. The 66th NVA Regiment (of the 304th Division) was the pride of "Uncle Ho" and Gen. Vo Nguyen Giap, a highly respected North Vietnamese military leader. Earning fame in 1965 for the battle in the Ia Drang Valley, the 66th was the first NVA regular army unit to engage U.S. forces. It stayed active in the II Corps area, including at Pleiku in 1967 and during Tet in 1968, although its fortunes changed after the United States entered the war.

Prior to 1965 the 66th fought mostly guerilla-type actions against ARVN troops, with great success. Large-scale actions were not its forte. Hence, the U.S. forces, which were superior logistically to the enemy in general, inflicted heavy casualties and significant strategic losses on the 66th. Nevertheless, the 66th supported the NVA Tank Battalion at Benhet in 1969 and 1970.

In 1970, the 66th was still the "go-to" unit to sweep Buprang and Ban Me Thuot into the control of North Vietnam. With all the losses and failures they had suffered at the hands of U.S. forces since 1965, military experts had cause to wonder why Ho Chi Minh and General Giap believed that the 66th NVA was their premier unit.

The NVA troops began taking up positions around the perimeter of the base. As it turned out, this maneuver was the first step in a strategic North Vietnamese plan to capture the Buprang Special Forces camp and use it as a springboard from which to seize the provincial capital of Ban Me Thuot and conquer the entire Dak Lak province. Kate was the first obstacle to this plan, and the North Vietnamese were fiercely determined to eliminate it.

Meanwhile, life went on at Kate. The adage about combat being long stretches of acute boredom punctuated by moments of sheer terror was proving true. That was about to change.

Specialist Fourth Class Nelson Frederick Koon noted that when he arrived at Kate on October 20, things were pretty laid back. He spent the days learning about the howitzer, "humping Joes" (carrying 155mm projectiles), cleaning his M16 rifle, playing volleyball, and performing whatever mundane tasks needed to be done. Koon's job was a prime example of what soldiers from time immemorial have laughed at when the army assigned MOSs (military occupational specialties). The army seemingly went out of its way to assign specialties that had little or nothing to do with soldiers' actual skills or civilian careers. If a soldier had been a chef, he might become a radio communications specialist. A surgeon in civilian life might become a cook. (Fortunately, the army never went so far as to assign a cook to be a surgeon. MOS assignments had their limits.)

Koon's original MOS was light weapons infantry, or 11B10. But when he arrived at Kate, it had been changed to cannoneer, 13A10. He was assigned to work with a 155mm towed howitzer crew of Charlie Battery, 1st Battalion, 92nd Field Artillery. He was learning on the job at Kate. As things would turn out, it did not matter what anybody's MOS was. When the long stretches of boredom punctuated by moments of sheer terror turned into six days of sheer terror, Koon and everyone else became basic infantrymen. They had to be if they wanted to survive. Their predecessors at Benhet had managed to do so a few months earlier. The defenders at Kate hoped to do the same.

Chapter 2

Benhet

"As far as the 1st Battalion 92nd Artillery History is concerned, the Dak To, Benhet, Dak Seang area is perhaps the most heavily fought over piece of terrain that the Battalion occupied."

—COL. BOHDAN PREHAR,
A BATTERY COMMANDER, SEPTEMBER 1968–MAY 1969

When Colonel Prehar uttered the words above, they may have been true—at least at the time. Members of 1/92 who fought at Kate several months later might have disagreed.

The siege of Benhet, which took place between May and July 1969, was a harbinger of the battle for Kate. The siege lasted for fifty-five days until friendly forces managed to lift it in early July.

Certainly, life was not easy at either place. But the troops engaged at Benhet had a few advantages over those at Kate, such as usable roads and more ground protection. In any event, Benhet provided some lessons for the friendly troops who would defend Kate three months after the siege of Benhet was lifted. Whether they were helpful was another story. Nonetheless, there was one major difference between Benhet and Kate: Benhet remained under allied control.

9

Benhet—and Been Hit

Benhet was the site of a Special Forces camp, 8 miles east of the tri-border region with Laos and Cambodia and 285 miles northeast of Saigon in the rugged Central Highlands. The troops' mission was to guard the tri-border area, protect the valley, and interdict enemy supplies and communications.

The U.S. Green Beret soldiers and artillerymen at the camp were supplemented by about 400 Civilian Irregular Defense Groups (CIDG) troops and supported by B-52 bombers, jet fighter-bombers, helicopter gunships, and artillery support from several nearby bases in the Dak To Valley. The men felt relatively safe at the camp. However, they did not believe the nearby firebases were nearly as well protected. Neither did the NVA.

The NVA decided to capture the camp—or at least keep it under siege while applying constant pressure to the firebases. The friendly forces had one major advantage over the NVA: air power.

Between May 6 and June 26, 1969, the NVA fired approximately five hundred shells of various types into the camp. They did not launch any ground assaults against it, with one major exception. The NVA attacked Dak To, the district capital, on June 1, but was repulsed. For the most part, the NVA reserved such attacks for the firebases, and even they were few and far between at the beginning of what became an eight-week siege.

June Swoon

Major battles were nothing new in Dak To. U.S. and ARVN troops fought a ferocious battle there in 1967 from November 3 to November 22 against People's Army of Vietnam (PAVN) units. On paper, the friendly forces won the battle. They drove the North Vietnamese from Kontum Province and practically destroyed the 1st PAVN Division.

After the battle ended, U.S. forces began to move out from the cities and lowlands. By the beginning of 1968, about half of all U.S.

combat units in Vietnam were operating outside these critical areas, which fit into the PAVN's objectives. In that sense, Dak To was a tactical loss for the friendly forces. However, they had not abandoned the area completely, as the battle between friendly forces and NVA elements on June 1 demonstrates.

North Vietnamese troops began their attack on South Vietnamese district headquarters at Dak To that day with a mortar barrage for cover as they attacked the 125 South Vietnamese militiamen defending the site. It took about one hour, but friendly bombs and artillery drove the attackers away. Two defenders were killed in the battle, four wounded, and half the headquarters site damaged. Nobody had an estimate of NVA losses since the NVA was not in the habit of releasing casualty statistics. The attack got the friendly forces' attention.

According to South Vietnamese estimates, one regiment and two Ranger battalions, comprising approximately 2,000 troops, were conducting Operation Dan Quyen ("People Rights") in the hills around Dak To. The objective of the operation was to alleviate the NVA's pressure on the area—and there was a considerable amount of it.

Friendly estimates suggested that there were 45 NVA battalions operating in the highlands at that point. That amounted to about 52,000 NVA and Viet Cong troops massing from bases across the border in Cambodia. Those forces were facing 89,000 American, South Korean, and South Vietnamese troops.

South Vietnamese troops were able to whittle down the number of enemy soldiers. They killed at least 216 NVA troops around the end of May and beginning of June, while sustaining 47 KIAs (killed in action) and 117 WIAs (wounded in action) of their own. Limited numbers aside, the friendly forces accomplished one significant objective: they broke the siege of Benhet and disrupted one of the NVA's favorite tactics, that of keeping the "puppets" bottled up by shutting down the roads in the area to prevent the camp and the firebases from receiving reinforcements and supplies.

The NVA's strategy worked for a while. By the end of June, the friendlies had had enough. They determined to break the NVA's stranglehold on the area and make life easier for everyone, especially the 1/92nd Artillery, which was manning the firebases in the area. Unknown to 1/92nd personnel, they would be placed in a similar situation at firebases around Buprang and Du Lac only a few months later. First, they had to get away from Benhet.

Something Wicked This Way Comes

As April 1969 gave way to May, troops in the Benhet–Dak To–Dak Seang area started picking up intelligence reports that indicated an NVA buildup. They were correct: two NVA infantry regiments and elements of an NVA artillery regiment were positioned south of Benhet, Firebase 6, and Dak To. Apparently, Dak To was their focus. The friendly forces began a buildup of their own.

Area administrators reacted quickly. Colonel Nguyen Ba Lien, the commander of the 24th Special Tactical Zone, established a Combined Tactical Operations Center at FSB 1 Dak To to control the troops being inserted into the area to counter the NVA threat. Lien was an experienced combat leader. He had led South Vietnamese forces at Hill 875 west of Dak To in October–November 1967 in what was considered the bloodiest battle of the war to that point. More than 700 Americans and 1,641 communists were killed there. He also commanded the South Vietnamese troops at Benhet in 1969, where 1,850 communist troops died during the siege. Lien was killed in December 1969 when a helicopter in which he was riding was shot down over a Central Highlands battlefield.

The commander of the 1st Battalion, 92nd Artillery, Lt. Col. Nelson Thompson, was designated the Fire Support Coordinator for the Dak To–Benhet area of operations. Thompson's Dak To Combined Fire Support Coordination Center mission was to control the fires of all U.S. and ARVN artillery in the area and coordinate all air fire, e.g., B-52 strikes and helicopter gunships. Eventually, the unit grew into the equivalent of one battalion group, which included forty-one tubes of field artillery and six air defense artillery twin 40mm M42s.

Thompson's command was active. Between May 4 and July 8, 1969, members coordinated more than 150,000 rounds of artillery, 1,100 sorties of FAC-directed tactical air strikes, 533 combat sky spots, and 142 B-52 strikes. In the same period, the 24th Special Tactical Zone employed nineteen maneuver battalions, with as many as nine battalions committed at one time. In addition, friendly forces killed more than 1,800 NVA troops.

Splitting the Difference

One of Gen. Robert E. Lee's favorite tactics during the American Civil War was splitting his troops to take his Union rivals by surprise. If that was good enough for Lee, it would work for the friendly forces around Benhet as well. They needed something to compensate for the growing complexity of their organization and situation. Thus, they established a battalion group on June 9, 1969. The forward command post remained at Dak To while the 6th Battalion, 14th Artillery, established a forward command post at Benhet. The commanding officer of the 1st Battalion, 92nd Artillery, was named the battalion group commander. In the long run, it did not matter who was assigned where. Everywhere they went, they were in harm's way. Both command posts sustained intense enemy fire, including from B-40 rockets and 75mm recoilless rifles and sapper (combat engineers who specialize in explosives, among other things) attacks.

June 1969 in particular was a difficult month for the troops at Benhet, during which a large number of well-armed and well dug-in NVA surrounded the camp. The NVA had the airfield and all established helicopter pads zeroed in with their firing data. They developed a well-practiced pattern. When an aircraft attempted to land, it received small-arms and automatic-weapons fire. Once it reached the ground, the aircraft was subjected to mortar and recoilless rifle fire. The friendly forces had no recourse when it came to utilizing aircraft. Large NVA ground forces effectively cut the road to Benhet, so aerial resupply was essential, as was artillery to negate NVA operations.

FOTs to the Front . . . To the Rear
. . . To the Side

Friendly units of all types operating in the Benhet area requested and received forward observer teams (FOTs) from 1st Battalion, 92nd Artillery, to support their operations. Between May and July 1969, FOTs were assigned to the 3rd Cavalry Squadron; 1st Squadron, 10th Cavalry; 1st and 4th Battalions, 42nd Regiment; 2nd and 5th Mobile Strike Force; 2nd and 3rd Battalions, 47th Regiment; 1st and 3rd Battalions, 53rd Regiment; and 11th, 22nd, and 23rd Ranger Battalions ARVN. One team was assigned to Dak To District to fire defensive targets for friendly villages. Two aerial observers were employed daily. Enemy artillery fire killed one 1st Battalion, 92nd Artillery, FOT member, SP4 Eric J. Greco of Headquarters Battery. He died in action on May 14. Greco was the first of many artillerymen who would lose their lives during the siege of Benhet.

Not only were FOTs dispersed throughout the area, but so were other units of 1/92. The 1/92nd Artillery forward command post was located at FSB 1, Dak To. Battalion headquarters and service batteries remained at Artillery Hill in Pleiku. A Battery was spread out as well, located at LZ Mary Lou near Kontum with the mission of general support reinforcing; A Battery Platoon was at Benhet doing the same. B Battery was located at FSB 6, 4.2 miles southwest of Dak To. C Battery was located at Landing Zone Bass, 13 miles west of Kontum, while C Battery Platoon was located at FSB 12, Benhet, 9 miles northwest of Dak To. Batteries moved around frequently as enemy activity increased. On May 4, A Battery moved to FSB 1 to supply general support reinforcing to 24th Special Tactical Zone Operations in the Dak To–Benhet area. Five days later, the base began taking incoming enemy fire every day.

During the next month, FSB 1 received 703 rounds of incoming 122mm rockets. One artilleryman, PFC Ronald J. Carter of A Battery, was killed in action on May 11 when direct hits from both a B-40 rocket and mortars struck the firing bunker he was in. The incoming enemy fire spurred the troops to adapt, improvise, and overcome—a philosophy that would be applied at Kate and its sister bases a few months later.

In response to the daily aerial attacks by the NVA at FSB 1, some bunkers were built with an overhang. That did not help protect the artillerymen completely. The one in which Carter was located when he was killed had an opening on top with two howitzers inside aiming west. The bunker withstood the attack, but shrapnel came through the opening on top, killing Carter and wounding several other men.

Two days later, a 122mm rocket landed approximately five feet from a manned howitzer. As a result, four men—SP4 Thomas M. Connell, SP4 Thomas W. Davis, S/Sgt. Donald R. Kraft, and PFC Lynn J. Wieser—were killed. Eleven others were wounded. The deaths and injuries were devastating, but they neither intimidated nor discouraged the men of 1/92 Artillery—which would also be the case at Kate and its sister firebases in the months to come.

Continue the Mission

There was no shortage of brave men in the unit. (There was a reason 1/92 was known as the "Brave Cannons.") Thirteen men volunteered from Artillery Hill, Headquarters and Service Battery, to replace the dead and wounded. They were airlifted into FSB 1 that evening. Their presence was welcomed since A Battery had been in action practically nonstop.

The battery operated under fire a good deal of the time, supporting the maneuver elements and returning accurate and effective counterbattery fire whenever Dak To was attacked. As the artillerymen fired, they received a large number of 122mm rockets fired by NVA troops into the Dak To compound. That, added to the recoilless rifle fire they received against their position, made their lives difficult but not untenable. After all, the troops they were supporting were in harm's way too—and in desperate need of artillery support

A Battery Platoon's mission remained general support reinforcing, with priority of fires to Benhet counterbattery. On May 27, A Battery was assigned to provide general support reinforcing, with priority of fires to the 2nd Ranger Group (ARVN), which was in continuous contact with the enemy. The NVA kept up the pressure on them, and friendly forces added to the confusion.

On May 28, a CV-2 aircraft resupplying Benhet by airdrop accidentally dropped a fifty-five-gallon drum of fuel oil on one of A Battery's gun bunkers. There were no casualties as a result, but the flash wall on the right side of the bunker was destroyed. That was one more obstacle the battery had to overcome.

May gave way to June. On June 2, A Battery's mission was changed to general support reinforcing with priority of fires to the 4th Mobile Strike Force Battalion. Two days later, A Battery Platoon's mission was also changed to general support reinforcing. Its assignment was also to support 4th Mobile Strike Force Battalion. That day, June 4, was a costly and tragic one for A Battery. Two members of the unit, PFC William C. Burgess and PFC David R. Porter, were killed by enemy fire. Three other men were wounded as a result of incoming 75mm recoilless rifle fire. That was an ominous sign for A Battery. It marked a switch in tactics by the NVA.

You Fire at Us, We Fire at You

In the first week of June, NVA troops doubled down on A Battery. They launched 122mm rocket fire at the base. Then, when A Battery manned its howitzers for counterbattery fire, the NVA directed recoilless rifle fire against its positions. This new strategy had an adverse effect on the American artillery units almost immediately.

On June 5, A Battery Platoon, 1/92nd Artillery, took a direct hit on a gun section bunker. There were no casualties, but one bunker was destroyed and needed to be rebuilt while A Battery was under fire. The following day, A Battery Platoon was hit again. The platoon took a direct hit on its powder bunker, which destroyed 560 canisters of powder. The devastating attacks continued when, on June 7, an NVA B-40 rocket hit A Battery's 3rd Gun Section bunker at Dak To and destroyed a flash wall.

The revolving mission assignments continued unabated. On June 9, A Battery was assigned general support reinforcing with priority of fires for one platoon of 2nd Mobile Strike Force Battalion. From June 8 to 12, A Battery Platoon conducted a daily "hip shoot" to enable it to fire counterbattery while Dak To was receiving incoming enemy fire. (A "hip shoot" is when an artillery unit stops at a clear area to set up its guns. A single gun fires one round to check aim and make corrections. Then the entire battery fires off rounds. Finally, the battery packs up and continues to its assigned position.)

Little changed for A Battery as the action around Benhet continued. It kept taking hits. On June 8, the FDC at Benhet received a direct hit, resulting in minor damage. Damage was more severe the next day, when six A Battery Platoon members were wounded in action by incoming 75mm recoilless rifle fire. Over a week went by before another soldier was wounded. He sustained wounds from mortar fragments.

Mission assignments went back and forth during that time period. Regardless of the mission and the units A Battery supported, physical damage to troops and equipment occurred. Between June 22 and 23, three NVA rounds struck three A Battery Platoon gun bunkers, causing superficial damage. But on the twenty-third, A Battery Platoon's powder bunker sustained a direct hit, which wounded five men. The resulting blast destroyed the bunker and 350 canisters of white bag powder.

A Battery crews were due a change of scenery. They got it, although the change was akin to transferring from the *Titanic* to the *Lusitania*.

On June 26, the crews of A Battery Platoon exchanged positions with the crews of C Battery Platoon, 1/92nd Artillery Dak To. The howitzers remained in place. The switch did not provide much of a change of scenery for the crew members, but it did unite them once again as a battery. After that they began to feel like they were on a treadmill.

On July 14, A Battery moved four howitzers to Artillery Hill to support the 3rd Battalion, 6th Artillery. The next day, A Battery personnel traveled via road to Landing Zone Oasis. From there, they went to Landing Zone Elaine. The battery's general support reinforcing mission included priority of fires to the 1st Squadron, 10th Cavalry.

Going to and fro did not stop the constant fire that was sent the battery's way by the NVA. It remained under constant fire throughout this period. Each time the battery carried out a fire mission, the NVA attacked it with all the weapons at its disposal. About the only consolation the gun crews had was that their counterparts in B Battery were subjected to the same harassment.

B Battery Gets Battered

B Battery, 1/92nd Artillery, was located at FSB 6. On May 4, the 24th Special Tactical Zone Force began operations in the area, supported by B Battery. It wasn't long before the battery sustained death and destruction.

The battery was engaged in a battalion time-on-target (TOT) and massing of fires mission on an NVA position close to FSB 6 on May 9. Suddenly, an explosion of the breech end of a howitzer killed one man, PFC Arturo S. Sisneros, and wounded six others, all of whom were medevaced successfully. The battery did not remain shorthanded long. Two days after the explosion, a howitzer from C Battery was brought in to replace the damaged gun.

Like A Battery, B Battery's missions changed frequently. The amount of damage it sustained did not. On June 8, sixteen incoming 75mm recoilless rifle rounds struck FSB 6. One round hit the mess hall while several landed on an ammunition bunker. Despite the damage, no one on the ground was wounded or killed.

Unfortunately, one UH-1 helicopter was hit during the first attack and crashed into its landing area. The losses did not go unavenged. Even though the NVA was inflicting damage on the friendly forces, it was paying a price of its own. Counterbattery fire from A, B, and C Batteries destroyed the NVA's positions. That only encouraged them to apply more pressure to the firebases with infantry attacks.

On June 11, an NVA infantry company with sappers attacked FSB 6 with small-arms fire, satchel charges, concussion grenades, B-40 rockets, 75mm recoilless rifle rounds, and mortar fire. The sappers exploded four satchel charges near B Battery's 6th Howitzer Section. The crew members were undaunted.

The gun crew continued to fire its howitzer throughout the attack. As it turned out, the battle was one-sided. Not a single B Battery trooper was wounded, although two of the CIDG defenders were injured. Conversely, twenty-five NVA soldiers were killed, and many of their weapons were captured.

C and Service Batteries

The remaining two elements of 1/92 contributed a great deal to the operations around Benhet. Like A and B Batteries, C Battery changed missions frequently and moved from place to place as the need arose. Among other locations, it had crews at Plei Ring De, an asphalt plant, and FSB Mary Lou to defend Kontum and Dak To and to provide general reinforcing support for the Dak To–Benhet area.

On June 26, C Battery Platoon's crew was airlifted into Benhet to exchange places with the crew of A Battery Platoon. The gun crews were interchangeable, which was a great benefit to the ground troops operating in and around the area.

Service Battery was just as flexible as the other three batteries. One of its most significant contributions was sending volunteers to replace the slain and wounded members of A, B, and C Batteries. It also maintained a flow of badly needed supplies to the other three batteries and fulfilled requests by the 52nd Artillery group to bring supplies to other units. Significantly, the 1/92nd Artillery was the only airmobile 155mm howitzer towed unit in the 52nd Artillery Group.

Altogether, Service Battery moved 198 tons of supplies by helicopter to A Battery, 1,740 tons to B Battery, and 703 tons to Battery C. The battery also brought in additional supplies via air and road. Although the number of tons sent to A Battery pales in comparison to the amount delivered to the other two batteries, it was a remarkable accomplishment nonetheless. A Battery was under constant daily attacks, which made deliveries extremely difficult no matter how they arrived.

Remarkably, throughout the siege, the 1/92nd Artillery's battalion surgeon managed to take care of the battalion's sick and wounded personnel and complete fourteen MEDCAP visits in conjunction with personnel from Headquarters Battery. (MEDCAP was the Medical Civil Action Program, under which U.S. medical doctors and specialists employing equipment and supplies set up temporary field clinics to provide limited medical treatment to the local population.) During those visits, 666 villagers received general medical care. Even under enemy fire, 1/92nd Artillery tried to keep the local population healthy while their own health was in jeopardy. Finally, they received some relief.

Sacking the Siege

On June 24, NVA troops fired about 110 artillery rounds and mortar shells into the camp at Benhet, which was occupied by 12 U.S. Special Forces advisors, 189 U.S. artillerymen, and hundreds of South Vietnamese regulars and CIDG forces. The bombardment continued the next day. The shelling was simply a continuation of the indiscriminate artillery attacks that had been going on for two months. The NVA forces were about to get a rude awakening.

A four hundred-member Mobile Infantry Strike Force ("Mike Force") was dispatched from nearby Pleiku and flew into Benhet on June 24. That same day, nine trucks from an eleven-truck ammunition convoy guarded by friendly forces arrived in the camp after traveling down Route 512 from Dak To, eight miles away. (The NVA destroyed the other two trucks as they passed.) The convoy succeeded in traversing the last section of the highway, known as "Suicide Mile," despite taking heavy fire from NVA troops in the jungle bordering the route.

Two U.S. Army Engineers and nineteen ARVN soldiers were wounded during the trip, but the fact that the reinforcements ran the gauntlet successfully was a positive sign for the friendly forces. (One source stated that two American soldiers were killed in the convoy, rather than wounded.)

The new arrivals went into action immediately. B-52s saturated the area with at least 180 tons of bombs on the NVA troops hiding in jungles about three miles south and two miles north of the camp over a two-day period. Following that, the Mike Force began a sweep of the area about one mile south of the camp.

The Mike Force was a reaction force composed primarily of Montagnards, Vietnamese, ethnic Cambodians, or ethnic Chinese. They were organized, equipped, trained, and led by U.S. Army Special Forces and Australian Special Air Service (SAS) advisors. At times, there were only one or two Americans or Australians assigned to a force of several hundred mercenaries.

It was difficult to keep the units focused on their missions, which included reinforcing Special Forces camps; conducting search and destroy missions and combat and reconnaissance patrols in force; and recapturing camps overrun by Viet Cong or North Vietnamese Army Regular forces.

The 5th Mobile Strike Force was a country-wide Mike Force. Fifth Mobile Strike Force Command kept one company of Mike Force troops on alert at all times. It could move a company of approximately one hundred fifty well-armed, well-trained combat soldiers within an hour of notification that they were needed in a combat area.

The troops met little resistance on their sweep at first, but by the time it was over, at least 183 NVA soldiers had died in the fighting around the camp and its outposts. Ironically, most of them were reported killed by artillery, which they had been fighting so hard to eliminate during their unsuccessful siege.

At last, the long battle at Benhet was over. Some of the friendly troops could breathe with relief. But their respite was temporary. Three months later, some of them were back on firebases in harm's way, and the terror began anew. The siege of Benhet had provided the friendly forces with a "lessons learned" scenario. That didn't make their lives at Kate any easier.

Chapter 3

Of All the Places in Vietnam . . .

"Success (victory for War and stability for Warfare) depends on destroying the will to fight of your opponent. This is only accomplished through neutralization of your enemies or adversaries, i.e., by causing them to convert, give up, or die. Those desiring Peace, but who are unwilling to pay the price to obtain Peace, do not understand this reality—they keep looking for a 'soft' way."

—SAM HOLLIDAY

In September 1969, 1st Lt. Reginald Brockwell attended a briefing conducted by his outgoing battalion commander, Lt. Col. Donald McNutt. (Later that month, Lt. Col. Elton Delaune would replace McNutt.) That was the first time Brockwell heard of the Duclap–Buprang campaign in Vietnam. He remembers that campaign today, as do many of its survivors, especially the men who participated in an escape-and-evasion (E&E) maneuver led by two U.S. Army Special Forces soldiers, Sgt. Daniel Pierelli and Capt. William Albracht.

The Friendly Lineup

Brockwell had been selected to do some initial groundwork constructing firing charts and looking at the fire plan for the area. IFFV Artillery would establish the Forward Mobile Staff in Ban Me Thuot. Provisional Artillery Group, which had all artillery units in southern II Corps under its command, would help establish firebases around Buprang and Duclap. This whole operation was set up as a showcase for the ARVN command to tout the results of "Vietnamization." Colonel Francis Bowers, commander of the Provisional Artillery Group, indicated that these firebases hacked out of the jungle for this mission were never designed as permanent locations. He was right: they almost didn't last long enough to be considered even temporary.

The NVA Team

The North Vietnam Army (NVA) 66th and 28th Infantry Regiments, along with elements of the K-33 Battalion, 40th NVA Artillery Regiment, the C-21 Company, K-37 Sapper Battalion, and the K-394 NVA Artillery Battalion, had moved south through Laos and Cambodia to the Duclap and Buprang vicinity, where arteries of the Ho Chi Minh Trail crossed into South Vietnam. These were major arteries leading to Saigon and Ban Me Thuot.

The NVA units were not strangers to Brockwell. Early in his tour in Nam, he had encountered them in the Benhet–Dak To campaign as a forward observer assigned to several U.S. artillery battalions from the 52nd Artillery Group (Pleiku), which was operating in concert with the ARVN 24th Special Tactical Zone (STZ). He would become far more familiar with them in the coming days.

Unfortunately for the friendly forces, Ho Chi Minh died on September 2, 1969. Ho's death prompted the NVA and its associates to step up attempts to drive the allies out of the area. At a memorial service on September 6, the North Vietnamese were encouraged "to turn their grief into revolutionary actions, uphold their resolve to fight, and ceaselessly cultivate their revolutionary ethics to outstandingly fulfill all tasks" in the Central Highlands. The NVA took these words to heart: "After a period of mobilizing all of our forces to carry out transport work on a line more than 70 km long, under torrential rain and B-52 carpet bombing, on the morning of 29 October, we began to attack and seize the Ka Te Base [LZ Kate], thereby kicking off a new offensive along the entire enemy defense line from Buprang to Duclap."[*]

---

* *People's Armed Forces of the Central Highlands during the Resistance War against the Americans to Save the Nation* (Hanoi: People's Army Publishing House, 1980), 186–87.

Brockwell's Role

Brockwell was one of the most experienced fire-direction officers in the Provisional Artillery Group (DaLat). He had varied experience in his battery, which consisted of 8-inch and 105mm howitzers, 175mm guns, and 81mm and 82mm mortars. While operating out of Duc-Trong, he had conducted artillery raids northwest toward the Buprang–Gia Nghia area, and he had been to the area as an aerial/forward observer. Significantly, Brockwell was familiar with another interesting point about Duclap and Buprang: when firing east from those locations, there was a map and grid convergence that had to be taken into account in any firing data.

There was another reason Brockwell had been selected for the mission: he had requested to interview for the position of general's aide for the incoming IFFV Artillery commanding officer, Col. Charles Hall. That request had unintended consequences for the young lieutenant—and almost cost him his life.

Entering the Escargot Pool

Brockwell's appointment had already been approved by his battalion and the Provisional Artillery Group. There was one hitch: Hall was not a general yet and did not need a general's aide. Until Hall's promotion became official, Brockwell had time to work on his assigned project while being interviewed and observed. Since he was at Duc Trong–Dalat, between Buprang, Duclap, and Nha Trang, the coordination would be easier.

His battalion, the 5/22 Artillery, also had its Bravo Battery in nearby Ban Me Thuot. During McNutt's briefing, Brockwell learned that the 5/22 Artillery would be coordinating platoons or sections from 5/27, 1/92, and 2/17 Artillery, spread over six or seven firebases in the Buprang–Duclap area. CIDG tribesmen advised by Special Forces teams in the area would provide their perimeter security. The plan seemed straightforward enough.

Brockwell underwent his first interview after he was pulled from a raid site and flown to Nha Trang in a somewhat disheveled condition.

He protested weakly to the deputy commander of IFFV Artillery that he was in no state for an interview. The protests of a lieutenant have all the power of a plea from a snail in a French restaurant to be spared from the escargot pool. The deputy commander told Brockwell that the colonel would appreciate seeing combat troops straight from the field.

Hall, We Have a Problem

Brockwell and Hall began the interview informally. They discussed family, duck hunting, and other items of common interest. Then they went into a briefing room. Hall showed Brockwell a plan that had already been developed. Initially, it consisted of three firebases in a triangle formation south and east of Buprang. Hall named the firebases Kate, Susan, and Annie, after his three daughters. Duclap had a similar configuration, with firebases named Helen, Martha, and Dory. The names sounded good to Brockwell. The plan? Not so much.

Brockwell thought he knew about the planned splitting of batteries for internal fire support to each firebase. Then he noticed something odd: the bases were very close to the Cambodian border. He asked if he was correct about the placement of the bases. Hall said he was and asked Brockwell what he thought about the plan.

The lieutenant knew that it really did not matter what he thought, but he offered his impression of the plan all the same. He understood fully that the triangular formation would let them fire artillery support for each other while supporting Buprang, but because they could not fire into Cambodia lest they create an international incident and because they would have only twenty-five to thirty U.S. artillerymen on each base, it seemed to him that the number of NVA in the vicinity could easily effect a siege against all three bases at once, as they had done at Benhet, in which case each base would be reduced to firing for itself, with no support for or from the others.

Actually, U.S forces were authorized to fire into Cambodia when exigency required it. According to a mid-November 1969 official statement from the headquarters of Gen. Creighton W. Abrams, the commander of military operations in Vietnam from 1968 to 1972, "The U.S. command has previously stated that if fired upon from enemy positions outside South Vietnam, U.S. forces are authorized to return fire. This is an inherent right of self-defense against enemy attacks." Abrams admitted that U.S. forces had already fired into Cambodia: "With respect to recent operations conducted in the Buprang area, some of the enemy artillery positions firing at Buprang were located across the border in Cambodia. Allied forces operating in the area have returned fire with artillery and tactical air strikes."

The deputy commander assured Brockwell that with air support, ARVN troops, and the Special Forces contingent, sieges would not be a problem. Outside of this unsettling piece of news, the interview went very well. Brockwell suspected that his concerns might not be a problem in theory, but the troops on these firebases were going to be faced with reality. It would be a problem.

Brockwell kept his feelings to himself. At that point he was feeling confident about everything—except finding himself on Kate, Susan, or Annie. Sure enough, he would end up on Kate.

"Kenn" We Hold the Place?

Like Brockwell, SP-4 Kenn Hopkins of the 1/92 Artillery had misgivings about Kate. He had been in-country for six months and had served at notorious firebases like Firebase 6, Dak To, and Benhet, to name a few. He knew from the start that this assignment was not going to be easy. "We were at a staging area in Ban Me Thuot when we finally received word where our next location would be and what configuration the battery would be in," he recalled. "Two guns would be going to each firebase, to include Annie, Susan, and Kate. My gun, a 155 howitzer, along with another gun from Charlie Battery, would be going to Kate; there would also be a 105 howitzer from another outfit. The other four guns of our battery would be split between Annie and Susan to provide overall fire support to Buprang and allow each of the other firebases to cover the other two."

That was all Hopkins had to hear. Kate was only a few klicks from Cambodia. He had heard there was an NVA camp that was also very close. He thought simply, "Man, I am no longer happy." He had reason not to be.

Quang Duc was at the end of the Ho Chi Minh Trail, a 9,940-mile supply route the Vietcong and NVA used to transport supplies from North Vietnam to South Vietnam through Laos and Cambodia. Construction of what became known as the Ho Chi Minh Trail began on May 9, 1959, well before the U.S. became involved officially in the Vietnam War. The trail consisted of a series of truck routes, foot and bicycle paths, and waterways. Friendly forces subjected the route to constant bombings throughout the war, but with limited success. The Vietcong and NVA were equally determined to remove any roadblocks along the trail—Kate among them.

The new firebases and the Special Forces camp at Buprang were blocking the NVA's logistical efforts. Thus, the NVA decided to eliminate the facilities in order to launch an all-out attack on Buprang, Duclap, Ban Me Thuot, and other bases in the area. An operational report from the 7th Cavalry, 17th Regiment, dated February 16, 1970, bears that out:

> The primary aim of the enemy's propaganda campaign was to discredit the GVN administration and the US Armed Forces. DARLAC province experienced relatively light enemy activity due to the shift of emphasis to the DUCLAP/BUPRANG area during this period. Harassing attacks in the vicinity of BAN ME THOUT City were the most significant enemy activities in November. On 16 November BAN ME THOUT City Airfield and the 23rd ARVN Division Headquarters received simultaneous attacks by ground fire. Minor attacks against the outlying hamlets of BUON DANG and BUON D'HAM occurred in early November. During December, US elements operating south of BAN ME THOUT City found 3 sizable caches of arms and munitions. A PW captured in the same area

on 25 December was identified as a member of the K394 NVL Artillery Battalion. He stated that the C-3 Company, K394 VNA Battalion was east of BAN ME THOUT City. The unit's mission was to transport rice to KHAN HOA Province.

Several sniping incidents were reported during December. Enemy activity increased in the Province during January. Major ARVN elements that returned to the area probably provided a more lucrative target for enemy elements to further their activities designed to discredit the GVN administration and its armed forces. Enemy elements conducted a sapper attack against an ARVN Regimental Command Post 10 kilometers north of BAN ME THOUT City on 6 January. This attack resulted in 9 friendly KIA, 20 friendly WIA and 6 enemy KIA. Elements of the 401st Local Force Sapper Battalion and the E301 Local Force Battalion probably participated in this attack.

These units constantly operate in the vicinity of the MWAL Plantation. The 303rd Local Force Battalion is another major enemy element operating in the vicinity of BAN ME THOUT. Enemy propagandizing and proselytizing activities increased during late January as the TET period approached.

(d) QUANG DUC Province: QUANG DUC Province was the scene of intense enemy activity during November and early December. Intense shelling forced the abandoning of Firebase KATE (YU573538) on 1 November. Firebases SUSAN (YU518439) and ANNIE (YU483513) were closed the following day due to the intensification of enemy activity in the BUPRANG area. (The YU . . . entries designate grid points on a map.) After all major firebases between DUCLAP CIDG Camp and BUPRANG CIDG Camp had been abandoned enemy forces concentrated their efforts on the two CIDG Camps and bases of supporting ARVN Units. Almost daily allied bases in the DUCLAP/BUPRANG area received significant standoff attacks from enemy elements employing an assortment of mortar, rocket and, in some cases, artillery fire. Elements of the 66th NVA Battalion supported by the K-33

Battalion 10th NVA Artillery Regiment and C-21 Company, K-37 Sapper Battalion were primarily responsible for standoff attacks and ground attacks against BUPRANG CIDG camps and RVN forces operating in the vicinity. Much of the artillery fired on BUPRANG CIDG Camp and Firebase KATE came from positions inside the CAMBODIAN border. Enemy forces operating in the DUCLAP/BUPRANG area sustained heavy casualties with the support of Tactical Air Strikes and Artillery to eliminate the active threat of enemy forces in the area. Friendly casualties were relatively light during most of the contacts with the enemy forces in the area. DUC LUP CIDG Camp and neighboring bases received 107mm and 122rn rockets, assorted mortars, limited ground probes. The 28th NVA Regiment and the K 39th NVA Artillery Battalion supported by elements of the K-37 Sapper Battalion and the 40th NVA Artillery Regiment were primarily responsible for attacks in the DUCLAP area. Antiaircraft units supporting enemy elements in the DUCLAP/BUPRANG area employed a highly formidable network of antiaircraft positions to interdict aerial support of friendly forces operating in the area. Several aircraft supporting operations in the area received hits from 12.7mm and smaller caliber enemy weapons. One of the more significant ground to air fire incidents occurred on 2 November. Three aircraft from B Troop, 7th Squadron, 17th Cavalry were shot down while conducting visual reconnaissance in the vicinity of Firebase HELEN (YU801635). Shelling attacks and ground attacks reached a peak in the later part of November. Due to the effectiveness of friendly operations in the area, enemy forces lost their capability to sustain themselves in repeated contacts. As December passed, enemy activity gradually subsided to the point of negligible contacts. Main force units withdrew to base areas inside the Cambodian Border. Since that time most of the major units involved in enemy activities in QUANG DUC Province were reported moving north toward PLEIKU Province and the Tri-Border area.

Although the emphasis of attacks w[as] in the BUPRANG/ DUCLAP area, there were also directed attacks against GIA NGHIA and KIEN DUC District Headquarters during the period. Except for small ground probes and harassing attacks by fire, enemy activity was at a very low level during January.

Moving Day

Between September 15 and 21, the various platoons and sections from the different battalions began to stage into their locations. Guns and crews were moved from their original bases to Ban Me Thuot, Duclap, or Buprang and then moved out to Kate, Annie, and Susan as air assets (helicopters) were available. As each base was occupied, a company of Montagnards with their Special Forces advisors was inserted.

Two teams occupied Kate: a company advised by Team A-233 from Ban Don with their Special Forces advisor, Sgt. First Class Santiago M. Arbizo, and a company from Team A-236 from Buprang, advised by Capt. Lucian L. Barham, the commanding officer of A-239 at Duc Lap. They secured the base's perimeter, and everybody settled in.

When Hopkins's unit arrived at the firebase, they set up the guns and then started building their fortifications. The crew members had to fill sandbags, create bunkers, and store and find protection for their "Joes" (a ninety-seven-pound projectile that came in a variety of configurations, from explosive, flares, or antipersonnel to powder canisters). They also had to dig in their hooches, small huts or dwellings used on a temporary basis. Building hooches may not have required a Frank Lloyd Wright to design them, but they could not merely be thrown up with no regard to safety and comfort, especially when the artillerymen planned to stay in one place for a while. It required considerable effort, depending on how deep the crews wanted them, how much of the structures they wanted above ground, how much or how little head room they were able to put up with, and what was available to support the sides and top. Fortunately, there were sandbags—lots of sandbags—available for their protection.

The 155s were placed in the southern part of the firebase, and the 105 was placed in a saddle to cover the jungle to the north. The west side of the firebase was very steep, and there was a ridgeline overlooking the base to the east.

Tactically, Kate Couldn't Be in a Worse Place

During the setup process, Hopkins noticed little things about the area. Their location, on top of a peak, had a nice saddle going off into the jungle, while the other three sides of the peak had fairly steep drop-offs. Two of the three sides were believed too steep for a ground attack by the NVA (which turned out to be a false assumption).

Hopkins was positioned with some Montagnards on the east side of the firebase, where the ridgeline to the east overlooked them. There was a small river forward of their position. The ridgeline that overlooked their location was within the range of his M79. He concluded that they were in a very poor tactical position.

The NVA held the high ground and was in a position to shoot down at Kate. The west side, which was opposite Hopkins's hooch, was very steep and went down the entire length of the mountain into a nice-looking valley that seemed to go on forever. It was a travel agent's dream, but an artilleryman's nightmare.

To someone looking down into the valley, an individual at the bottom would look no larger than an ant. The jungle started about fifty yards from the top on all sides of their location. The south side, which was opposite the saddle, was also very steep, and the ridge across from it was also higher. Going left to right, it dropped off sharply into the same beautiful valley.

Everyone Is Ready except the NVA

Everything at Kate went smoothly at first. It looked like Hall might have been right about the safety of the bases. There was little activity on the firebases except the normal fire missions in support of Camp

Buprang and its patrols. There was a simple explanation for the inactivity, as later intelligence explained. The NVA had not done a reconnaissance of the area for several weeks and was unaware of the three new firebases. Once they discovered the firebases' locations, things changed quickly.

On October 27, Sgt. Dan Pierelli, a twenty-two-year-old Special Forces soldier, relieved Sergeant First Class Arbizo, who had been in-country almost a year, starting with A-233 on October 23, 1968. (He would serve almost two years, departing Vietnam on September 22, 1970.) Pierelli, like Arbizo, was fairly experienced by this time. He had served with the 5th SFGA from March 1969 and was a dedicated Special Forces soldier. As he averred later, "I can honestly say that I have never had the pleasure of meeting greater people than those I served with in Special Forces. They had integrity and dedication that is all too often missing in our society today."

The next day, Capt. William Albracht, the executive officer at Buprang, arrived to relieve Captain Barham, who had come to Kate from A-239 at Duclap. Barham, who had been with A-239 since May 23, 1969, was leaving for R&R. Remarkably, Albracht was a year younger than Pierelli. He took a circuitous route to get to Kate, but as he said, "Fate—she cannot be denied."

Albracht's Route to Special Forces and Kate

In officer candidate school, everybody applied for units. Every unit for which Albracht applied was Special Forces. When he joined the U.S. Army at age eighteen, he was too young for Special Forces; enlisted members had to be a minimum of twenty years old. There was no such restriction for officers. After OCS graduation, Albracht completed jump school at Fort Benning, Georgia, and then reported to the 3rd Special Forces Group at Fort Bragg, North Carolina.

When Albracht reported to Fort Bragg, administrators asked him if he wanted to go immediately into the Special Forces Officers Course (SFOC), which was starting the next Monday. That was a break for him. The SFOC was difficult to get into, and the waiting list was months long. Albracht jumped at the chance. He started the course in mid-September 1967 and graduated on December 15, 1967.

The training was tough, but he was fresh from OCS and jump school, which helped him get through the physical part fairly easily. Mentally, SFOC taught Albracht how to think outside the box. The next logical step for him was to put his new skills to the test. Like all good second lieutenants did at the time, he volunteered for Vietnam. His brother was already there with the 5th, but Bill didn't think it mattered. Besides, he did not end up in Vietnam right away.

Albracht was assigned to the 46th Special Forces Company (1st SF Group) in Thailand, where he spent the first six months as the S-4 (logistics officer) at a B-team camp, Non Takeo. He spent the next six months at an A-camp in southernmost Thailand, this time as the executive officer. His primary duty was to help train the Royal Thai Army.

About a month before his yearlong assignment in Thailand ended, Albracht offered to stay another year, but only if he could go to Vietnam with Special Forces. The officer he spoke to looked at Albracht with the same look the recruiter had given him when he had enlisted in 1966. "This, my friend, is your lucky day!" he told Albracht.

The young second lieutenant took a thirty-day leave and then deployed to the Republic of Vietnam—finally. When he got there, Albracht asked to go to the Mike Force. But he had no combat experience, so the army denied his request. It was ten months before he got that experience, at Kate. The man who had learned to think outside the box in SFOC would need every trick he had acquired—and then some—at that godforsaken firebase.

Albracht took over as senior ground commander at Kate. His arrival coincided with the NVA's recognition of the threat posed by the firebases and their determination to address it. Before the siege ended, it would involve thousands of NVA troops, scores of helicopters, U.S. Air Force gunships and jets, and a U.S. Army Special Forces relief force, not to mention deaths, injuries, MIAs, medals, and bravery galore. The battle for Kate became a significant struggle for survival that was seemingly of little or no interest to anyone at the time except to the soldiers involved.

Day 1

October 27, 1969

Chapter 4

Sergeant Pierelli Arrives

"Once men are caught up in an event, they cease to be afraid. Only the unknown frightens men."

—ANTOINE DE SAINT-EXUPERY

Sergeant E-5 Daniel Pierelli, Special Forces advisor to the CIDG company at Trang Phuoc–Ban Don and weapons specialist, arrived at Kate to replace Sergeant Arbizo. His timing was fortuitous. The artillerymen there had limited, if any, infantry training. They were not quite prepared for attacks from bugs or enemy troops. It was his job to get them ready.

Let the Volleyball Tournament Begin

Pierelli had a hard time believing what he was seeing when he arrived at Kate. Security was lax, and the troops seemed more like they were at a resort than a firebase. That was partially true, but more because they were bored with, rather than negligent about, security.

Hopkins explained what had happened since his arrival. After the artillerymen finished setting up, they were ready for almost anything,

"If one could ever really be ready to get hit." But, when nothing happened, the troops at Kate settled into a somewhat enjoyable routine. Any thoughts of enemy attacks moved to the backs of their minds.

The artillerymen started their mornings by filling empty powder canisters with water and placing them on top of the powder bunkers so they could have sun-heated warm water to bathe with. There was always a volleyball game at some point during the day in which the best players from the two 155 sections or the 105 section competed against one another. Hopkins does not remember which side was dominant. All he remembers is having a good time.

All that leisure time was strenuous. The troops worked up heavy sweats, which only a good bath could relieve. So they started each evening with a "whore bath," since the water from the powder canisters was always warm by that time and a bath was welcomed. That warm water seemed to remove much of the dirt and grime of the day's activities and relaxed the men just enough to allow them to enjoy the exceptionally beautiful sunsets they witnessed from the top of the mountain.

Going Buggy

The days of rest and relaxation had to come to an end. Finally, there was an attack on the base—from bugs. During their first week on Kate, the troops fell victim to a vicious assault by small, gold bugs. As Hopkins described the critter, "It was about a quarter of an inch and sucked your blood; everything in Vietnam seemed to want your blood in one way or another."

Every day for three days, the bugs arrived in the late mornings. They began their assault up the south side of the firebase in a swarm, landed on anything containing blood, and started biting. The troops at Kate learned quickly. After the first day's attack, as soon as the swarm appeared, the soldiers all ran for cover. But the first wave of gold bugs was simply an advance unit. The troops could not do much more than joke about the critters.

Let Peace Reign

The peaceful conditions that existed at Kate in the early days of its existence gave the troops a chance to mingle and get to know one another. Hopkins became friendly with some of the Montagnards, or "Yards," and occasionally invited them to play volleyball with the troops. The Americans traded their C-rations to the Yards for some of their food, just for a change in diet.

Every once in a while, the Yards took Hopkins on excursions down into the jungle. They visited a small river located some distance down the mountain. While the Yards filled their canteens, Hopkins just looked around in amazement and enjoyed the jungle scene. He did not give much thought to what might be lurking in that jungle, nor did anyone else.

Hopkins's misgivings about the location of Kate were falling by the wayside simply because it all seemed so peaceful, especially when he compared it to the other locations he had been assigned to since arriving in Nam.

Our Defenses Are Down

Pierelli was not deceived by the apparent calm that pervaded Kate. He got right to work. A Camp Strike Force Company from Trang Phuoc was supposed to follow him and rotate with another company on October 28 from the same camp that had been at Kate for a while. That did not happen.

The new company arrived all right, but sixteen CIDG members of the unit being relieved had to stay at Kate to bolster the security force. The troops' comings and goings were transparent to Pierelli. He had an immediate need to strengthen the security at the firebase. Pierelli occupied himself for the rest of the day by organizing his troops into their new positions. He knew that one day was not nearly enough to improve security, nor could he do the job alone. When Albracht joined him the next day, he went to work in earnest.

Day 2

October 28, 1969

Chapter 5

Captain Albracht Takes Command

"You have never lived until you have almost died.
For those who fight for it, life has a flavor
that the protected will never know."

—U.S. ARMY SPECIAL FORCES SAYING

Two momentous events occurred hours apart on October 28: the NVA launched its first attack on Kate and Captain Albracht arrived to assume command.

At about 11:30 A.M. that morning, lead elements of the NVA infantry, which outnumbered Kate's defenders by about forty to one, opened a preliminary assault with intense small-arms fire from all compass points. One of their first targets was Ambush Hill, an elevated listening post about 110 yards from Kate's perimeter. The incoming fire from the NVA was so overwhelming that the post's half-dozen defenders had no choice but to withdraw to the comparative safety of the base.

Captain William Albracht arrived at Kate around 3 P.M. The newly-minted captain was just twenty-one years old. Kate was his first command. It would come close to being his last.

Albracht did not want to be there, but not because of the dangers inherent at an isolated firebase. He was a professional soldier; danger was part of the job. Rather, he believed he could be more valuable at the Special Forces camp at Buprang, where the troops were preparing for an imminent siege predicted by intelligence sources. Kate was not part of that situation. Little did Albracht know that he might have been better off at Buprang.

There Is Someplace Else I'd Rather Be

The captain had protested to his B Team commander, Lieutenant Colonel Simmons, that he "did not want to go sit on his butt at Kate when there was work to be done at A-236." His argument fell on deaf ears. Despite the perils the troops on the firebases faced, army routine had to be followed.

Dutifully, Albracht boarded a chopper from Buprang to Kate to relieve Barham. The change-of-command ceremony was brief and informal. They exchanged a few pleasantries, and Barham provided a brief overview of the situation at the base. Then Barham quickly—and happily—boarded the chopper, departed for R&R, and left Kate to its fate. Albracht remembered, "As I cleared the backwash of the chopper, I looked over my shoulder and saw Barham wave as he jumped on the same bird I had arrived on."

Albracht's arrival meant more than a new commanding officer for the troops. He brought a culture change. Hopkins recalled that whereas Barham "only seemed to want to party and play volleyball, this new captain, William Albracht, wanted to 'tighten up' the place a little too much." The laid-back conditions on the base might have been acceptable when there was no reported enemy activity in the area, but by the time Pierelli and Albracht arrived, the situation had changed.

The Numbers

The base's personnel roster on the afternoon of October 28 was not very impressive in number. It comprised Pierelli and Albracht, two Vietnam Special Forces members, a Camp Strike Force company of about a hundred men, and the sixteen members from the relieved company who had stayed behind. There were also a forty-man Camp

Strike Force platoon from Detachment A-236, Buprang, and the reinforcement platoon from the U.S. 5th Battalion, 22nd Artillery. The artillerymen had at their disposal one 105mm gun and two 155mm howitzers. Pierelli and Albracht knew how many men they had. They did not know how many NVA troops were out in the nearby jungle waiting to attack. They simply prepared for the worst.

Intelligence suggested that there were numerous NVA troops in the area. Sources revealed that the 46th NVA Artillery Battalion was located twelve miles north of the CIDG camp at Nhon Co. They also claimed that some of the NVA troops wanted to go to Chieu Hoi (loosely translated as "Open Arms"), a joint U.S.–South Vietnam psychological operations program initiated in 1963 that invited North Vietnamese soldiers to come over to the South Vietnamese side.

Friendly recon troops had captured documents on October 10, six miles east of Camp Plei Me, that showed that the 40th Artillery Regiment had split into two regiments, 40A and 40B. The 46th Artillery Battalion was subordinate to the 40B NVA Artillery Regiment.

Intelligence experts suspected that the 40A Artillery Regiment was operating in the northwestern part of the II CTZ (Corps Tactical Zone), while the 40B Artillery Regiment was in the southwestern area. That meant clearly that the NVA had the capability of artillery support along the entire Cambodian–Laotian border in II CTZ. The troops at Kate would learn soon enough that the NVA artillery existed—when rounds started raining down on their positions.

One Special Forces agent had learned about a Vietnamese civilian who had been driving a Lambretta on Highway 14, twelve miles south of Camp Buprang when an unknown number of NVA soldiers stopped him. According to the driver, they told him that there were about three hundred NVA soldiers in the area, probably from the K-37 Sapper Battalion. They added that they would attack somewhere around Kien Duc, eight miles northwest of Camp Nhon Co, between November 3 and 6. Forewarned is forearmed, as the adage goes. Albracht was both.

The Games Are Over

Under Albracht's command, there would be no more volleyball and the life of leisure would be gone. Although his 3 P.M. arrival meant he was too late to do anything but make a thorough inspection of the perimeter and defenses before nightfall, Albracht did not waste any time beginning the process.

As soon as he dumped his gear, the captain met the sergeant. He and Pierelli walked the perimeter on a detailed inspection to get a feel for security and operations on the base. By the time they had noted all the perimeter's vulnerabilities, night was falling. The two Special Forces soldiers made plans to begin fortifying their positions the next day.

Albracht asked Pierelli about patrols. Pierelli revealed that Barham had allowed the Yards to "go hunting" in the immediate area around Kate, but these were the only patrols at present. Both soldiers felt these patrols were inadequate, so they decided on a strategy to implement directed saturation patrolling the next day. But they were hampered somewhat in how they assigned patrols.

"I never had a chance to increase the patrols around Kate," Albracht explained. "I arrived on the afternoon of October 28 and the attack started that night. The first real patrol was on the morning of October 29, when Dan (Pierelli) and I went to access and investigate the attack on Ambush Hill the night before."

Most of the troops available to Pierelli and Albracht were Montagnards. They were CIDG strikers from Camps A-233 and A-236. They provided security for the twenty-seven artillerymen from elements of the 1/92, 5/22, and 5/27, although Hopkins disputed that number of artillerymen. "I know there were only four people in my 155 section," he said. "And I think there were five in the other 155 section and five on the 105." He speculated that the other artillerymen were associated with the fire direction control. None of them had seen any action at Kate. They got a chance to utilize their skills that night, but it was not the first action of the day at the base.

The Action Begins

During the day, after an excursion to the nearby river, Hopkins loaned his artillery section's M60 machine gun and some ammo to the Montagnards. After they set up the gun, a Yard noticed some movement in nearby trees. They opened up on the location with the machine gun. It may have been nothing, but at least the Yards got to test the machine gun. (They probably *had* seen something, as later events proved.)

That night, the Yards on patrol established an ambush site on a hill between Kate and the Cambodian border. Later, the hill, which became known as Ambush Hill, would feature prominently in the E&E operation during which the troops left at Kate would barely escape with their lives. The hill, about 880 yards to the north of Kate, had been cleared for fields of fire down the base's north-northwest slope to a gap in the triple-canopy jungle at the bottom. There was a clump of trees on top of the hill. The rest of the hill was covered in waist-high grass.

The base, by contrast, was surrounded by jungle. There was another hill on the north side of Kate. To reach Ambush Hill from the second hill, troops used a gap in the jungle eleven to thirteen yards wide. That gap is where the Yards established their ambush—and where the fighting began.

Midnight

Around midnight, Ambush Hill erupted with an intense volume of automatic-weapons fire and grenade explosions. Several of the artillerymen were sitting around talking and listening to music when the sound of small-arms fire erupted in the distance. They ran immediately to their gun pits in anticipation of orders for a fire mission. The call came down for some illumination rounds in the direction of the firefight as the Montagnard patrol made its way back to the base's perimeter.

Quickly, the Yard strikers on the patrol came running back to Kate. "Beaucoup VC," they kept saying when Albracht and Pierelli debriefed them: "Many enemy." They discovered later that what the strikers had encountered were not Viet Cong (VC), but the lead elements of the

66th and 28th Infantry Regiments of the North Vietnamese Army, with the 40th NVA Artillery Regiment in support.

Albracht did not care particularly at that point whether the enemy troops were VC or NVA. Either way, they posed a serious threat to Kate. At that moment, he had absolutely no intelligence to indicate the size and type of the enemy units probing their operational area. But it would not be long before he found out that the NVA had been building up its forces and planning an attack on Kate for some time. That time had come, and Albracht's decision to increase patrols around the base had paid off. He decided a little extra help would be welcome, too.

The captain called in a Spooky to work in a full circle around Kate and Ambush Hill until about 2 A.M. The artillery's 105 howitzer and 155s also poured fire on Ambush Hill and the surrounding area.

Meanwhile, there was growing concern at other firebases in the area. The attacks on the bases started on October 28, but they were sporadic at first. They grew more serious early in the morning of October 29, when the enemy resumed its firing on Kate at about 8:20 A.M. Albracht would have liked a gunship overhead, but the entire area was in turmoil, and assets were limited.

A Shadow Covers the Area

There had been a flurry of activity in the area on the night of the twenty-eighth. At about 6 P.M., operations staff officer advisor Major Burr requested all-night coverage for Annie from Shadow. Half an hour later, the officer of the day at division tactical operations center, Tan Linh–Nhon Co, confirmed that Shadow would be on station. There was no apparent hurry to get it there, however.

At 8:30 P.M., a staff officer called Capt. Thomas J. Sardy at division tactical operations center, Tan Linh–Nhon Co, to find out when Shadow would arrive. Sardy did not offer any information. Another ten minutes passed and a second call went into Sardy. This time, the caller requested that Shadow be expedited. There was growing concern that the attacks were accelerating and the firebases were in danger.

The operations officer set up a teleconference with Lt. Col. Elton Delaune of 5/22 to ask that Dorrie be reestablished with a 175mm gun. Delaune advised them that Lt. Gen. Charles A. Corcoran, IFFV commanding general, would be attending a conference in Gia Nghia the next day, and the request might be considered.

Then another cause for concern surfaced when the reports came in from Kate regarding the Yards' contact with enemy troops and their withdrawal into the base's perimeter.

Taken in context, the contacts with the NVA on the twenty-ninth were not significant in nature, but they created a sense of foreboding among the firebase personnel in the area, and rightly so. The next few days would support suspicions that the base was in for a rough ride.

Day 3

October 29, 1969

Chapter 6

Crack! Boom!

"A close friend of mine was on the 45th Div. staff of Gen. P. T. Ginder, and he confirmed to me that reports from the front were many times ignored or put in classified status to avoid news media scrutiny or making PT's resume building a factor! So is the disgusting, void, and distorted communications of war."

—WAYNE PELKEY, KOREAN WAR "MUD DOG"

C rack! Boom!

Hopkins was not sure what the loud noise was that awakened him abruptly on the morning of October 29. Somehow he knew it was not a good sound. Indeed it was not. The NVA began the morning with its own version of reveille, which was to become a pattern at Kate. The enemy launched a "Good morning, Vietnam" mortar attack that got the defenders' attention.

At first, Hopkins thought the noise he heard was a 105 firing, but the sound of a projectile from that gun was more a *whoosh* than a *crack* or *boom*. He got out of his hooch to determine what the noise was. To his dismay, he saw that something had hit his 155. Hopkins looked down the hill and saw a series of holes on the 155's side. The holes ended at a discolored point on the tube of his gun.

Enemy gunners had used a basic technique to hit the 155. The ridge from which the NVA gunners was firing was higher than Kate's top. They set up a recoilless rifle, a direct-fire weapon, and walked rounds up the side of Kate until they hit the 155. Their position gave them a decided advantage. Even though there were protective parapets around the 155s, the guns were exposed to anything firing from above. That explained why Hopkins's gun was knocked out of commission on October 29. Score one for the NVA.

"Game on," Hopkins thought to himself.

So it was. That was the day the NVA accelerated the fighting around Kate. Although NVA after-action reports exaggerated the outcome of the battle at Kate, and in the region in general, they were accurate in one respect: the NVA caught the derided puppets' attention.

A Transformation Occurs

The early-morning noise also woke 1st Lt. John Kerr, the fire-direction officer for C Battery, 1/92 Artillery.

SP-4 Bob Johnson was on the radio in the fire direction center (FDC) when the incoming started. Kerr ran to the underground FDC to see what was happening.

"Better go get your rifle," Johnson said

Kerr ran back to the sleeping bunker, where he found his sleeping bag full of holes, with down feathers everywhere. Lieutenant Mike Smith, the executive officer of Charlie Battery, 1st of the 1/92 Artillery, and the only other artillery officer at the base, got shrapnel in the nose during the barrage, which led to his removal from the firebase a short time later. That left Kerr in charge of the artillery.

Troops all over Kate recognized quickly that they were under full-scale attack.

The explosions rocking Kate roused Specialist Koon out of his fitful slumber, too. Like many of his comrades, he believed that they were the sounds of his own guns firing. Then he wondered, "If they are ours, why am I not on my gun?" He did not have time to ponder for long. When Koon heard someone yell for the medic who was assigned to the artillery unit, he realized they were under attack.

Koon made an instant transformation from artilleryman to infantryman. Since the gun he was assigned to had been hit by a B-40 rocket or an RPG (rocket-propelled grenade) and put out of commission, he grabbed his M16 rifle and headed for the perimeter. When he arrived there, Albracht was on the radio calmly calling for gunships, close air support, and fire missions from Firebase Susan.

The gun crews on Susan responded with alacrity. Barnes stated that the guns on Susan fired incessantly 24/7, alternating back and forth to give Kate support in fighting off the siege, especially when it came time for the E&E. They fired so often, in fact, that the crews had to change gun tubes at Ban Me Thuot later when they finally left Susan.

Even though Francis Barnes was not involved in the E&E from Kate, he empathized with the troops who were, for the same reason his comrades from all the supporting units did: they were fellow soldiers who were in trouble and needed help. "From all accounts I heard, it had to be a very harrowing and stressful time for the command and soldiers on Kate," Barnes said. "I only fired support and prayed to God for my friends and others on Kate."

At least he had the opportunity to fire guns on their behalf. Many others could only pray. There was plenty of that going on, locally and back in the U.S., where newspapers printed daily accounts about the sieges. At Kate, the troops needed all the prayers they could get.

Okay, Now What Do We Do?

"With all the mortars and rockets exploding around us, it was pretty natural for us to duck or flinch," Koon observed. "Captain Albracht was pretty much taking things in stride and remaining calm."

"How can you stay so cool?" Koon asked the captain.

"That is the way we are trained in Special Forces," Albracht said matter-of-factly.

That was the point when Koon realized Albracht was in complete command of everyone at Kate—and that they were in good hands. He wondered, though, if that was enough to keep them safe.

Their brief conversation over, Albracht turned to assessing the situation. He and Kerr were sitting in a foxhole, looking at one another and asking, "What are we gonna do now?" It was a rhetorical question. After Smith's evacuation they were the only two officers left to take command, and both did what they had been trained to do.

Even though Albracht had been at Kate only seventeen hours and Kerr had spent all his time in FDC rather than on the guns, they formed an instant bond. Kerr assisted Albracht as much as possible while the captain directed airstrikes during the day. The jet pilots supplying support were not making Albracht's job easy.

Cool Your Jets

At one point, the pilots were essentially demanding a body count of enemy troops from Albracht to justify their time on station. Enemy body counts were used in military reports and news reports to demonstrate progress in this war, so the pilots wanted to know if they were being "productive." Kerr felt sorry for Albracht as he tried to convince the pilots to stay without a body count. There was no time to conduct one, and it was not possible to get one anyway, considering the jungle growth and steep terrain between the NVA and Kate.

Albracht's call for help did not go unheeded. In addition to the jets, helicopters and gunships came and went. Kerr spent most of the day on the radio trying to coordinate supply helicopters and gunships. But he did not know who they were or what to tell them since it was not part of his regular duties. The fact that one of the responding gunships was shot down just outside Kate's perimeter made his job even more difficult.

Meanwhile, troops were carrying out whatever tasks they could. Artillerymen received orders to prepare the damaged 155 so it could be lifted out by a chopper. They were told that a replacement might be brought in. That did not seem too likely, since the continuous pounding from NVA mortars, rockets, RPGs, and small-arms fire prevented replenishment from air. Worse, enemy firepower hindered the landing of medevac choppers for picking up the wounded, one of whom was Albracht.

Kate Becomes a Beehive of Activity

The number of injuries was increasing along with the high volume of rocket and mortar fire. One of the first troopers wounded was an artilleryman who was hit in the back by shrapnel. The trooper ran to Pierelli and Albracht, who noted that he was bleeding badly. They realized that it wasn't a life-threatening wound, so they patched him up and refocused their attention on defending the base.

Albracht and Pierelli assembled a patrol of about forty strikers and set out for Ambush Hill to check out the enemy activity from the previous night. The point man maintained his normal interval of about fifteen yards ahead of the main body, while Albracht took a position as the third or fourth man back from the front. As they moved through the waist-high grass, Pierelli maintained the rear guard and kept the flank security at a proper distance.

The point man led the group through the gap on their approach to Ambush Hill. They veered to the right before reaching the top. There they found an NVA helmet and a blood spoor, which they followed toward the woodline to the northeast, the spot from which Ambush Hill had taken fire the previous night. Suddenly, one or more concealed machine guns and many assault rifles opened up on them from all compass points about thirty-three yards inside the woodline while the platoon was still in the open.

The platoon low-crawled to the meager defensive positions in a tree line to the east of the hill and started to return fire. In reality, they had only concealment, not cover, which increased their exposure to enemy fire. The troops began low-crawling toward a neutral woodline to their right (east). Once they got there, they regrouped and discovered that three patrol members had been wounded and one was missing.

Around noon, Albracht radioed for air support, which Capt. John Strange of Pterodactyl 10, part of the 185th Recon Aviation Company, answered. Albracht requested gunships, which arrived shortly thereafter, and asked Strange to look for the missing striker.

Before Strange could reach the site, a light observation helicopter (LOH) arrived. The pilot, described by Albracht as "a crazy man, no doubt," had picked up the radio traffic and offered to help in any way he could. He was as good as his word.

As the platoon started through the jungle on a flanking maneuver against the active enemy positions, the "crazy" LOH pilot, whose identity still remains a mystery to Albracht, flew low over the enemy to draw fire, expending what little ordnance an LOH carried. The pilot even fired out the cockpit window with his .45-caliber pistol. He warned Albracht by radio that large numbers of enemy were attempting a flanking maneuver to encircle the patrol.

The captain immediately ordered the troops to pull back in the direction of Ambush Hill in order to gain the tactical high ground and to better direct the air support that was now on station. As they were leaving the woodline and heading up Ambush Hill, one of the pilots advised that the missing Yard had been located. He was lying in tall grass, apparently wounded or dead, in the area of initial contact.

Albracht told Picrelli to cover him with M79 and M16 fire. He took three Yards and headed toward the downed striker while the patrol members provided cover fire. When they reached him, under increasingly intense fire, they found that he was still alive, but dying from a grievous head wound.

The captain ignored the almost certainly fatal nature of the head wound and hoisted the wounded man on his shoulders in a fireman's carry. He raced back to the platoon's line under a virtual rain of NVA fire, protected only by the friendly strikers' covering fire. As the rescuers neared their perimeter, a couple of Yards dashed out to meet them and took the wounded man from Albracht, only to discover that he had died during the carry. The deceased Yard was not the last man who would die in Albracht's arms before the siege was over.

Creating an International Incident

The LOH pilot and Captain Strange advised Albracht that his platoon was facing a vastly super-iron (i.e., well-armed) enemy force that was both entrenched and mobile. Based on that information, the captain requested additional air support. To his dismay, the radio coordinator told him that the next available support was twenty minutes away. That was an eternity as far as Albracht was concerned.

The enemy was obviously trying to insinuate itself between Ambush Hill and Kate to cut off the platoon's return to the firebase. Worse, the patrol members were low on ammo and had four seriously wounded comrades to carry. Albracht decided intuitively to withdraw to the more strongly fortified position back at the firebase before the NVA succeeded in cutting off his access. He did not realize the wisdom of his decision until later, when he learned that his patrol had been facing substantial portions of the NVA's main body of infantry which, by the end of the day, had completely surrounded Kate's perimeter.

The patrol averted the NVA's attempt to cut it off and made it back to the base. But, the members weren't any better off there. No sooner did they arrive than the incoming began again—and accelerated. It was only 10 A.M.

NVA gunners poured unrelenting fire from 82mm mortars, recoilless rifles, B-40 rockets, RPGs, machine guns, small arms, and grenades onto the base. Later, evidence emerged that some of the fire poured onto the base came from 85mm, 130mm, and 105 howitzers located in Vietnam and on a tea plantation/Cambodian Army base in Cambodia known as Camp Le Rolland, located about four miles from Buprang. The plantation, which was clearly visible on the horizon, served as an assembly point for the NVA throughout the battle.

Albracht was well aware of the fact that some of the artillery fire was coming from across the border. He did not particularly care. All he knew was that the artillery was endangering his troops. Consequently, he declared a tactical emergency and directed jets into the supposedly "neutral" country of Cambodia to bomb the heck out of one of its army bases.

"That actually created an international incident," he acknowledged. But his concern for the well-being of his troops overrode geographical boundaries. If the enemy wasn't going to respect those boundaries, Albracht wasn't going to either. Besides, the boundaries weren't clearly established.

There were several areas along the South Vietnam–Cambodia border that were not mapped clearly. The Buprang region was one of them. As a result, the maps the friendly commanders were using in the area were imprecise. So Albracht, like his command counterparts, could rationalize that they were simply firing on a target without knowing exactly in which country it was located.

Albracht was beyond caring about nuances. His main concern was protecting his troops. The captain asked for artillery fire on a target. The politicians back home could worry about the nuances.

Speaking Lattin

Enemy gunfire had a devastating effect on Kate. It had knocked out one of the base's 155 guns and the 105 howitzer. It became a constant struggle to keep them working over the next few days. Antiaircraft fire from the NVA's 37mm guns and .51-caliber machine guns heightened the dangers for the chopper pilots.

There wasn't much to bolster the defenders' spirits, but one bit of good news helped. Albracht had USAF air liaison Maj. George Lattin from Gia Nghia and several other army and air force observation planes on station to help control artillery and air strikes. B Troop 7/17 Cavalry choppers from Gia Nghia provided hunter-killer teams. For the next four days, Lattin was Kate's primary forward air controller (FAC), and he served as the defenders' virtual lifeline. He was one of many.

Other USAF FACs who worked the Kate area included Lt. Karl Gustke, Lt. Jeff Geagley, and Lt. Walter Phillips. Army FACs who were also heavily involved included Capt. John W. Strange, Lt. David Teague, and WO William J. Schaefer. Capt. Mike Leonard worked out of Gia Nghia shortly after Kate. He was Major Lattin's replacement.

According to Albracht, "Without TAC (Tactical Air Command) air, we would have been destroyed the first day, but Lattin personally made sure that we got all available fighters. He placed himself in danger on numerous occasions while directing his aircraft to keep the NVA at bay. The TAC air fighters, known as Boxers and Blades, were magnificent in their efforts."

Albracht kept in constant touch with the air support personnel. He worked TAC air during daylight, then worked Spooky from dusk into the night and early morning.

Never Let a Good Firefight Get in the Way of Bureaucracy

Despite the constant barrages raining down on Kate, the defenders managed to medevac the wounded and dead strikers. They had to be replaced somehow. Albracht requested additional manpower and received a promise of a company of Yard strikers from A-234 (An Lac). His request set off a round of bureaucratic maneuvering that could have had deleterious effects on the defenders at Kate had not reasonable heads prevailed.

According to the (CTZ) Mobile Strike Force–Kate After-Action Report, the first request for reinforcements was logged in at 1225. Captain Ramey of division tactical operations center (DTOC) advised that B-23 had strikers available at An Lac as reinforcements and requested that DTOC furnish aircraft to transport them. Ramey advised that the light command post—the site where the ground commander had set up—at Gia Nghia had to coordinate all such requests.

Major Burr confirmed Ramey's statement and added that "Personnel at this location are not in control of situation and will not accept requests for aircraft or other support." This set off a debate about who, if anyone, was going to reinforce Kate. Meanwhile, the base's defenders were still catching hell. Their lives were on the line while captains, majors, and colonels away from the base argued about command authority. The request for reinforcements went up the chain of command as Kate was going up in flames.

Company B CRT radioed a demand to Mobile Strike Force HQ that it furnish aircraft to extract the troops at Kate as soon as possible. HQ responded that it did not have any aircraft available. That revelation prompted a response that HQ advise Lieutenant Colonel Irrazzri that they were not supporting the troops properly. The bureaucratic sparring continued.

Does Anyone Understand the Severity
of the Situation?

HQ notified the 23rd Division that A-236 was moving into its area of operations and advised Captain Ramey that A-234 Opn C-251-A was standing by on the landing zone as an available reinforcing force. Ramey had Gia Nghia on the line and passed that information to the light command post.

There were other ongoing concerns regarding the firebases. Telecom Capt. John M. Nicola, liaison officer at light command post, noted that the crane assigned to remove the artillery from LZ Susan was en route to the Dak Sak area and required smoke cover. To complicate matters, Buprang A-236 was receiving continuous 82mm fire at a time when A-236 advised that security was on its way. About the same time, Maj. Pierre Kieffer III of Company B advised Nicola that An Lac troops were available to reinforce Kate. That created another snag.

Colonel Morgan took the phone and stated emphatically that Kate did not appear to need reinforcements at that time. How he knew that from a distance was unclear. He further declared that An Lac Opn C-251-A should never have been inserted into "his" area of operations without clearance through light command post.

Captain Richard L. Whiteside entered the fiddling-while-Kate-burned scenario. He advised Colonel Morgan that it was CTZ MTF's understanding that A-231, A-233, and A-234 were to continue conducting normal operations within their areas of operations since they were not OPCON (operation and control) to division at the time. Morgan apparently did not agree.

The colonel informed Whiteside emphatically that An Lac was—and always had been—his area of operations. Further, he stated, he would direct the removal of Opn C-251-A as soon as possible, but he had not yet determined where the troops would be taken or who would furnish the aircraft for the extraction. The debates about areas of operations, individuals' responsibilities, and so on were irrelevant to Albracht. He was still engaged in a life-and-death struggle at Kate.

Chapter 7

The Captain Takes a Hit

*"A man's work is in danger of deteriorating when
he thinks he has found the one best formula for doing it.
If he thinks that, he is likely to feel that all he needs is merely
to go on repeating himself . . . so long as a person is searching
for better ways of doing his work, he is fairly safe."*

—EUGENE O'NEILL

Despite the air support around Kate, it was obvious that the base was surrounded and its troops were outnumbered significantly. Chopper pilots were doing their damndest to help the troops on Kate— and taking heavy fire in their attempts. There was some confusion between the pilots and commanders on the ground regarding what was happening at Kate. Everyone was trying to find a better way to protect Kate, but they seemed to be working against one another at times.

Pat Ewing, a.k.a. Blue Star 144, was a pilot with the 48th Assault Helicopter Company Blue Stars, which was working with gunships called Jokers to provide resupply and reinforcement of Kate. He pointed to the differences in what commanders away from Kate were seeing and what the chopper pilots were experiencing. "I recall a level of confusion between what we were observing as we were inbound and what command was telling us through their directions and information," Ewing commented. "At one point I even remarked that they must have the map upside down since it seemed that they were acting on info that was diametrically opposed to what we were hearing on the FM frequency from the firebase and observing from the air as we were making our approaches with fresh troops." The attempts to resupply and reinforce Kate were fraught with danger for the pilots.

Gunships were receiving heavy automatic-weapons fire from a ridge west of Kate. The NVA's fire impeded choppers that were transporting badly needed supplies, including forty-five cases of smoke grenades, M-26A-1 ammunition, fragment grenades, and thirty cases of M79 high-explosive rounds. Amidst all the confusion, about forty reinforcements air-assaulted into Kate before the intense ground fire prevented any more sorties. The heavy fighting created a need for medevac choppers as injuries continued to mount.

Bringing in medevac choppers was a dangerous job for the pilots and ground troops alike. Whoever directed the choppers had to do so from open ground, in plain sight of the enemy. The exposure increased the defenders' risks, and there were a few narrow escapes. Rather than put his troops' safety at risk, Albracht chose to direct the incoming helicopters himself.

Late in the morning, Albracht was in the open guiding in a medevac chopper when he spied the distinctive launch of a B-40 rocket from a nearby hillside. His first instinct was to take cover, but to do so would mean the almost certain loss of the chopper, its crew, and the wounded troops it was evacuating. The medevac pilots were intently watching Albracht instead of the surrounding terrain. They had no way of knowing they were about to be hit.

Albracht waved the chopper off frantically. It got away just in time. Unfortunately, he was not as lucky. Shrapnel from the rocket hit him in the left upper arm. That did not deter him from continuing his activities. He considered himself lucky. Although Albracht eventually received a Purple Heart for these wounds, he steadfastly refused to be evacuated for treatment, then or later. At times, in fact, he even shielded the other wounded troops with his own body as they lay exposed to fire while waiting for the helicopters. He had little choice. Even at this early date in Kate's short history, there was little other cover left for the defenders inside the base, whose surface structures had been largely demolished by the enemy's light and heavy machine-gun fire, recoilless rifle fire, rocket-propelled grenades, and air-burst artillery.

Albracht continued to direct choppers in throughout the remaining days on Kate, but he was not hit again. Unfortunately, one of the most essential resources on the base was: the water trailer. The temporary loss of the water was just one more hardship the troops had to bear. (A helicopter later dropped a replacement water trailer on the base.)

Call Me Chicken

At one point during the day, when the incoming was particularly heavy, Albracht was trying to establish contact with a temporary FAC while Major Lattin refueled. Albracht heard a new voice and a new call sign on the air. The caller, obviously an FAC, was attempting repeatedly to contact whoever used the call sign "Chickenhawk." Albracht was a bit puzzled: his own call sign was "Chicken Wolf." He thought it was odd—and confusing—to have two such similar call signs in an area of operation where both could be heard on the air.

The incoming lessened slightly, but it continued to rain down substantially. Albracht waited for the FAC to contact Chickenhawk, but he could not raise him. Then it occurred to him that the FAC might be trying to contact him, using the wrong call sign.

Albracht raised the FAC and asked him if he was in fact trying to contact Chicken Wolf. The new FAC laughed and said, "Sorry, Chicken Wolf, I thought your call sign was Chickenhawk."

The captain replied, "You can call me Chickenhawk, Chicken Wolf, or Chicken Shit—just get me some TAC air in here now!"

That was the point at which his call sign changed immediately to Chickenhawk. The name was shortened even more after a while to just plain Hawk, which stuck for the rest of his Vietnam tour and beyond.

"We're doomed"

Koon was one of the troopers watching when the shrapnel entered Albracht's left arm. As soon as Koon realized the captain was wounded, he figured they were doomed.

"We'll be in a world of hurt without him," he thought.

Once he learned that Albracht refused evacuation, Koon speculated, "I guess he figured that he knew the situation we were in. He was there when the battle started and he was going to see it through till the end. He was going to get us all safely out of that hellhole or die trying."

Of course, Koon hoped for the former, as did everyone else. The outcome was in doubt at that juncture, though.

For the most part, the artillerymen could only sit and wait. It was harrowing, to say the least. Hopkins began the day staying close to his damaged gun. That first night under fire had been a restless time for him and the other troops. Like them, Hopkins had gotten very little sleep and did not want to go back into his hooch. He felt safer close to his gun, whether it was operational or not. Heck, he figured, it was already damaged, so why would the NVA want to hit it again?

Hopkins also recalled being taught in advanced individual training at Fort Sill, Oklahoma, where Army artillerymen were trained, that the worst thing a soldier can do in combat is stay inside a hooch or bunker. "You cannot see what is coming at you and it ensures you will be overrun," the lesson went. His training kicked in.

Like everyone else, Koon was antsy and wanted to be useful in some capacity. Doing something—anything—would help take his mind off the incoming. So he left his gun and went around checking on people, talking to them about what they knew and how they were feeling. When he reached the 105 section, they told him they were going to get another 105 brought in, since their gun was also damaged during the initial attack the previous morning.

Next, he and a few of his crew members checked on the one 155 howitzer still working. The crew loaded the gun to test-fire it on the ridge across from the base at a point where it dropped down to the valley below. To be on the safe side, they created a long lanyard, backed away from the gun, and pulled it. To their surprise, the round struck the ridge and caused a secondary explosion.

They had randomly selected a point not knowing or thinking there was anything there. After that, they informed everyone that at least one 155 was available for support. That was a morale booster, if nothing else. The troops needed every bit of support they could get.

Speaking of Lucky Shots

Koon and one member of the 105 crew, Michael Norton, both carried M79 grenade launchers as their personal weapons. They got together to look at the higher ridge facing the east side of Kate. Norton saw movement on the ridge, so they both fired their M79s.

All movement stopped after the rounds hit. A few seconds later, Norton fired again. As the projectile sailed through the air both soldiers saw an NVA "low-crawling." A second later, the M79 round struck the enemy. Koon and Norton jumped up yelling, "Got ya!" Every bit of success, however minor, was beneficial to the besieged defenders' morale at that point.

The pair went down to Norton's gun to inform his crew what happened and to receive congratulations. Retaliation was not long in coming. Koon was returning to the top of the hill when he heard a whooshing sound over his head. He looked up and saw a red object going over him. His reaction was unusual. "I remembered watching war movies and the zigzag you were supposed to do when being fired at," he reported. "So, I immediately started running up the hill to get to the top, zigzagging all the way. I thought to myself, 'Man, you probably look silly running like this.'" But, he added, "It did not matter since I made it up to some of my guys and the protection of some sandbags."

Of course, his buddies were not going to let the moment pass unnoticed. They told him that it looked like a scene out of a movie, with Koon running up the hill with a recoilless rifle shooting at him. A little comic relief was welcome at that point, but there was nothing humorous about the situation on Kate, which would grow more serious as the day went on.

Landing without Touching the Ground

Late in the morning, a chopper arrived to medevac Lieutenant Smith. It was a poignant moment for Koon, since Smith had been one of the officers in his advanced infantry training unit at Fort Sill. The medevac went off without a hitch. Shortly after the chopper left, another one came in with a colonel aboard. As Koon and the medic approached it, the colonel asked how they were doing. The medic asked him to take some of the wounded on the chopper when he left, but the colonel refused. The pilot took off without even touching the ground, much to the chagrin of the defenders. Unlike the success Koon and Norton had enjoyed earlier, this event did not do much for the troops' morale.

A short while later, yet another chopper touched down. The new artillery commander, 1st Lt. Ronald A. Ross, jumped out. Kate may have been under serious attack, but army protocol was still in place. Officers came and went in the midst of a battle in an effort to keep the chain of command in place. Ross had come to replace Smith. His stay at Kate would be short, as it turned out to be his last assignment. It should have been someone else's. Ironically, 1st Lt. Tom Klein, a close friend of Ross's, was on standby to go to Kate. The change in plans was a last-minute decision. It had a lasting effect on Klein, who wrote that "[Ross] had the biggest heart of anyone in the 5th Bn, 22nd Arty, and he was the most popular junior officer."

Koon got to talk to Ross before the lieutenant reported to Albracht. Ross told Koon he was supposed to be on his way for R&R to see his wife. But he had somehow "pissed off" Lieutenant Colonel Delaune, who sent him to Kate instead. (Ross's official biography says he volunteered for the assignment at Kate.) The base was a far cry from R&R, as anyone there could attest

Lamenting the Loss of Ross

John Ahearn, a member of the 155th AHC, was the pilot who delivered Lieutenant Ross to Kate. It was not a mission he relished, with good reason. "I remember a lot of time spent between Duc Lap, Gia Nghia and Buprang," he noted. "I do absolutely believe that the worst experience I ever had was resupplying the firebase Kate out east of Buprang late one afternoon." That was the flight on which Ross arrived, as Ahearn related in his account of the mission:

> I was in Ghia Nhia refueling and got sidetracked to go off to the Bu Prang area. An FAC told me to hold north of there and

await an Arc Light strike. I was told very specifically to get away from the vicinity of Kate. Based upon that order, I climbed to what I considered an altitude safe from any ground fire, several thousand feet up, and flew a holding pattern along an imaginary east-west line, north of the area.

I recall seeing the B-52 strike on the ridge line south of Kate and was just amazed at the east to west rolling thunder. All of a sudden, the earth erupted east to west on a ridge line just south of the firebase. It was totally amazing to see!

Immediately thereafter, a Chinook with a sling load tore out of Bu Prang with some Falcons covering it. I remember the pilot screaming on the radio as he flew into Kate and saw the crew kick off the sling load—short of Kate. In the immediate circumstances, it was very understandable why that happened. The Chinook was still at Ban Me Thout the next morning, with some big holes in it.

It was then my turn in the barrel, and the Falcons asked that we convene in Bu Prang. There, I was told they could cover me going into Kate, but they were out of mini-gun ammo. They assured me they could cover me with rockets, though.

Off we went out of Bu Prang with a load of small-arms ammo and an artillery officer, who was the new battery commander. I was definitely scared, but knew we had to go in there.

I remember being certain I was flying faster than the Charlie models and distinctly breaking across the forest area on to the burned-out, browned-out area around the base of Kate. I did a cyclic climb up and in, in what might have been the crappiest approach I ever made. However, we got in, the ammo got kicked off, and the new battery commander jumped off.

I flew down the side of Kate and turned toward Ban Me Thuot, while staying low on the trees. I recall very vividly that we just had stone silence for about ten minutes as everyone on board was just speechless. Finally, I climbed to some altitude and we made it to Ban Me Thuot uneventfully.

Upon arriving there, it was pitch dark, but we refueled and put the aircraft in a revetment. The next morning, Bill Melvin looked me up and gave me a royal verbal kick in the ass, due to some ventilation (bullet holes) in the tail boom we had not noticed in the dark. Some thought it might have been Falcon shrapnel under my tail feathers.

I believe that my co-pilot that night was Marlin Johnson. If not him, then it had to have been David Lichtbach. I seem to recall that the battery commander might not have survived the outcome of Kate.

Apologies to Eugene O'Neill

The defenders on Kate knew the feeling behind the title of Eugene O'Neill's play *A Long Day's Journey into Night*. As the day dragged on, the firing continued. But they got in a few hits of their own.

At one point, Hopkins and Pierelli inspected the perimeter of the base by dashing from position to position. That was the only way they could check on the troops, since the enemy could see every move they made, except during the dark hours. As they did, they saw movement in the valley below.

Pierelli called for an air strike on that location. It was an amazing sight for Hopkins, who swears he will never forget seeing the concussion wave when the bombs hit. After the blasts, they could not see any more movement. There was plenty of it elsewhere on the base, though.

Toward the top of the base, on the west side, which Hopkins thought was too steep for a ground attack, there was indeed such an attack taking place. Pierelli and Hopkins dove into a bunker, which they found already occupied by the medic and a few Yards. Again Pierelli called for gunship support.

The planes came in and raked the area with gunfire. The troops developed a routine. As the gunships passed, they would pop up and fire. Hopkins admitted that he was so confused and scared that he popped up at the wrong time and received pieces of shrapnel in his arm. When some of the pieces bounced off, one of the Yards patted him on the back and said, "You Number One. I stay next to you," as if Hopkins was a lucky charm.

Hopkins had to laugh, despite his pain. He thought, "If he only knew how confused and scared I am, he would not want to be within a mile of me."

The medic informed Hopkins that the wounds on his arm were worth a Purple Heart, which he thought was silly. Two years later, he was still picking out pieces of shrapnel.

Chapter 8

In a Fog

*"As Dustoff pilots in Vietnam, our task was to insure [sic]
that timely medical care was delivered to the wounded—a job that
was probably helped along by having a bent for
foxy flying and being a button short."*

—ANONYMOUS DUSTOFF PILOT

There was an extraordinary mission pulled off by chopper pilots late in the day of October 29. Extraordinary achievements by chopper pilots were becoming so common at Kate that it was hard to distinguish what was remarkable and what was routine.

Heroes in Helicopters

Around dusk the 155th AHC's Falcon 2 and Falcon 9 gunships had no sooner returned to Ban Me Thuot than they were called back to Kate to cover Dustoff 63, which was en route there to pick up five wounded. One of the injured was a Yard who had been wounded by a sniper while he manned a listening post. He was being brought back in to Kate from the listening post. The others were artillerymen who had been wounded when their gun was knocked out.

The weather was not conducive to flights of any type. There was a heavy fog that inhibited the pilots from seeing what was going on and coordinating with the ground troops directing them in. As Dustoff 63 circled Kate waiting for the striker to be brought back from the listening post, it began to run low on fuel. Finally, everyone was ready, and troops talked the Dustoff into the pad. Just as it landed, one of the advisors heard NVA rounds leave the tubes and yelled, "Incoming mortars! Get out, Dustoff!"

The Falcon gunship pilots could not see anything through the fog, so they were helpless to lay down suppressive fire. Suddenly, the Dustoff pilot, in an excited, high-pitched voice, yelled, "Dustoff 63 coming out to the east." Immediately, three mortar rounds impacted.

Falcon 2 asked if they were going to try to go back in. Happily, Dustoff 63 responded that he did not need another try. In those few seconds, the crew had loaded five wounded and gotten away without a scratch.

The pilot of Falcon 2, Les Davison, remembered it the same way:

The sun's last rays were fading as we refueled our Charlie model gunships for the sixth and last time (or so we thought). We were five minutes from shutdown, the end of a *long* day. Just as they had done during the monsoon season last year, the bad guys had come across the border from their Cambodian sanctuaries and were hitting hard at the Special Forces camps at Buprang and Duclap. We had launched before dawn and had flown continuously all day, stopping only to rearm and refuel. Our asses were dragging! The last thing I wanted to hear was my call sign on the radio.

"Falcon 2, this is Operations." I recognized the voice as Captain Giordano, the 155 Assault Helicopter Company operations officer.

"This is 2, go ahead."

"Are you able to go back out to LZ Kate to escort Dustoff for a pickup?"

LZ Kate was one of the artillery firebases near Buprang, the scene of heavy fighting. We had expended there twice during the day.

Pause. I wanted to say no. I looked over at Falcon 9, our trail ship. Jack Coonce had heard, anticipated my question, and signaled a thumbs up.

"We're on our way, Ops," I replied.

"Roger, 2. Contact Dustoff 63 on company uniform. Good luck. Operations out."

Dustoff escort was a familiar mission. We regularly went out with the unarmed Hueys. 63 was Denny Harrell, a good pilot and good friend.

As soon as we lifted off, I called 63.

"Thanks for coming out, 2. Spooky can't be on station until 2230, and the guys on the ground are hurting."

"No sweat, 63, we need the night time," I responded.

Crew chief Dave Nachtigall groaned, but every one of us knew that we wouldn't have let the Dustoff crew go out alone. The Red Cross markings did not deter enemy gunners in the slightest.

It was about forty-five minutes to Kate, and the ride was mostly a quiet one. We had been *so* close to shutdown, and all of us had begun to unwind from the day's tensions. Both our Falcon crews were trying to get on edge again as we flew toward the firebase.

Twilight was long gone as we passed near Duclap. There was a little horizon, but not much. It happened so gradually we didn't seem to notice—and then it was just all gray outside and the rotating beacon was flashing off the gray into the cockpit. What the . . . ?

"Break left Falcon 9, we're in the soup [fog]. We're coming around to the right on instruments."

I instructed Peter Pilot Bob Maddox, "Kill the beacon and watch the instruments with me. I haven't done this since flight school. You guys in back watch for ground reference." (Peter Pilot was a term used for pilots who were new to the unit or to the country. There were two pilots in a Huey. One was the aircraft commander, known as the AC, and the other was the copilot, also known as the Peter Pilot.)

We turned OK, and broke out within a minute or so, but it sure seemed like a long time. I never knew you could start sweating so quickly. From the back came, "Nice goin', Mr. D." That was quite a compliment from Cal Serain, the quiet door gunner.

We rejoined with Falcon 9 and headed west, at a somewhat higher altitude this time. Now we started to see patchy ground fog forming, and it was getting thicker as we flew on. I can't speak for the others, but I was certainly back on edge!

Twenty minutes later, we were orbiting over LZ Kate. More accurately, we were orbiting over the fog over LZ Kate. We listened as Dustoff 63 talked to the U.S. advisor with the ARVN artillery unit, Captain Albracht.

"It's been pretty quiet here since sundown. A few mortars and some sporadic AK fire, mainly from the west. One of our listening posts just took sniper fire; they're bringing in another badly wounded ARVN. Estimate arrival in 15 mikes. Counting him, we've got 5 WIAs," he told Denny.

"Roger, we're ready to pick up. I can see your light, but this ground fog may be a problem. We'll just hang around up here a bit. Let us know when you're ready."

Fifteen minutes later, Denny was told the wounded man was about ten minutes from LZ Kate.

"Falcon 2, say fuel?" he asked.

"Two's got 700 pounds. Falcon 9?"

"Nine is just under 800." A bit more than lead, just like the book says. Well done, Jack.

"63, this is 2. We're OK for a little bit."

Of course it was more than ten minutes; it always was. I was just about to call Bingo when the advisor told 63 that all five wounded were finally ready for pickup.

"OK, we're coming in," Denny replied immediately. "Keep your light on. Copy 2?"

No way we would leave now.

"Roger 63. I'm not sure we're going to be of much use to you with this ground fog," I said.

"That's OK, it makes me feel good just knowing you're around. Here we go."

Denny blacked out, descended, and hovered down the light. The stuff those Dustoff guys did was unbelievable.

We listened as the advisor talked the Huey in to the PZ. Then, just a few seconds after touchdown, we heard him scream into the radio, "Incoming mortars! Get out, Dustoff!"

I sensed rather than saw Bob flip the Master Arm switch to "Hot," which he confirmed over the intercom even as the advisor finished his warning. But, a quick check found that none of our Falcon crews had seen any tube flashes through the fog. Without targets, we could do nothing but wait. The mortars would be impacting any second. Come on, Denny.

"Dustoff 63 coming out to the east!"

Denny's voice had risen a bit. Seconds later, three mortar rounds flashed in the darkness.

"Falcons are at 2,500 feet directly overhead, watching for you," I called.

"We're breaking out, 2, coming up bright flash," said Denny.

"Contact," I told him. "Are you going to try again?"

I might have heard a chuckle.

"Don't have to. We got 'em."

"You picked up five in that time?" I was incredulous.

"Yep, those guys down there have got their stuff together. Let's go home."

Amen.

The U.S. advisor thanked Denny and his crew profusely as we turned east and climbed out.

Four hundred pounds, forty-five minutes; it was going to be close. Bob took the controls for the flight back. Fifteen minutes later, we saw the lights of Ban Me Thuot.

I called in. "Operations, Falcons 2 and 9 are inbound, ETA is three zero. Lead is a little short on gas; this one is going to be real close."

The fuel gauge showed 250 pounds.

"Understand 2. Keep us advised," said Captain Giordano.

The Dustoff ship was lighter and faster than our Charlies, so it was quite a way ahead of us.

"Falcon 2, this is Dustoff 63. Weather is good all the way back. We're switching to tower freq now. Thanks again for coming out."

"Great job, 63, call us anytime. See you in the club."

Click, click.

The first flicker on the twenty-minute light. Ban Me Thuot still looks a million miles away. I can't stand it. I'm so tense I have to do something, so I take the controls back from Bob. Then comes the CO's distinctive voice.

"Falcon 2, this is Stagecoach 6."

Major Owen had been a gunship pilot during his first tour. He knew who was flying late, and who might be in trouble—and he cared.

Just under 150 pounds.

"This is 2, go ahead."

"Do you want us to send a slick with fuel to meet you on the road?"

A night landing to an unsecured area, with lots of flashing lights from two helicopters: not my idea of a good time.

"Ah-h-h, you might have them start getting ready, just in case, Stagecoach 6. We're about two zero out, and the fuel light just came on."

"Roger 2, we're standing by," came back Major Owen.

Except for the whine and the whop-whop, it sure is quiet in here.

"Chief, how far has anyone gotten into your fuel light?"

"Captain Cunningham used eleven minutes coming back from Happy Valley, but that was in the daytime." No one laughed at Dave's joke.

Twelve minutes into the light: eight minutes left. There, I can see the lights on the landing strip. Bouncing just under 100 now. Is that gauge accurate? Oh me, oh my, pucker factor is *way* up.

It's funny, the things you think about. I'm back with the Air Force recruiter, and he's telling me to stay in school, get my degree, and then I can come fly with them. I should have listened, I could be doing 500 knots right now . . .

Sixteen minutes. I hate to, but I dogleg just a bit south to avoid the most heavily populated areas of the city and angle in to the strip from high above. Fifty pounds, give or take. We're high and fast on the approach, just in case—but it's so fast that we shoot right past the taxiway turnoff! It takes almost all of the 2,500-foot runway to get stopped.

I'm soaked in sweat, shivering cold, and nearly frozen on the controls as we settle onto the runway. Nobody says a word. We made it.

Nearly eight hours until the next mission.

Spooky in the Night

Night finally arrived. It did not make anyone feel better. Albracht and Pierelli knew that. They distributed some strobe lights for the troops to place around the perimeter. Pierelli told them to dig a hole and place the strobes in the ground so the lights would shine up, but not out. He explained to them that Spooky and other types of aircraft would be supporting them at night, and they needed to know where the perimeter was so they would not hit the defenders.

As strange as it seemed, that was the first night that some of the defenders actually got a little sleep. Spooky provided a considerable amount of protection overnight with its mini-guns. Granted, as Hopkins commented, it was a fitful sleep at best, "but any sleep was better than no sleep."

Kerr oriented two strobes on a north-south line. He stayed up all night on a handheld radio, guiding the high-flying gunships with their mini-guns as they attempted to keep the NVA at bay. Even they weren't safe from the enemy troops concentrated mostly on the high ridgeline to the east and Ambush Hill to the north. At 7:40 P.M., Shadow 51 arrived at Kate.

Shadow 61, already on site, received automatic-weapons fire approximately 550 yards north of Kate. It expended 18,000 rounds and 20 flares, with unknown results. At least they weren't hitting their own troops.

And the Arc Light missions provided by B-52s in the area provided a bit more cover and heightened the troops' sense of security, since they operated with a safety zone around Kate. (Operation Arc Light was the code name for B-52 missions carried out across Vietnam from 1965 until the end of American participation in the war in August 1973. The planes, carrying conventional weapons, conducted bombing raids of enemy base camps, troop concentrations, and supply lines.) They dropped 2,000-pound bombs "danger close" at Kate. ("Danger close" suggests that bombs were dropped as close to friendly ground troops as possible without hitting them. The distance depended to a large extent on the friendly forces' maneuverability.)

Kerr remembered clearly talking to the pilots, who were able to provide solid fire support without hitting the defenders' location. He felt good about being able to do that. But, when the gunships left at dawn, the incoming resumed. Neither Kerr nor anyone else realized how large the enemy force was and how much real trouble they were in. Intelligence reports revealed what was coming.

According to an S-2 (intelligence) analysis, "the attacks-by-fire and light ground attacks around Kate were probably conducted by unidentified regimental and battalion size units reported to be operating in the area." The troops on Kate might have disagreed: to them the attacks seemed anything but light.

The same analysis included a prophetic statement: "This greatly increased enemy activity in Buprang's tactical area of responsibility indicates that a threat to the camp and fire support bases is rapidly building." Furthermore, S-2 warned, there was a strong probability of continued attacks in the Buprang and Camp Duclap areas. S-2 earned its money with that report.

Day 4

October 30, 1969

Chapter 9

A "Black" Day for 48th AHC

"He who thinks of the consequences cannot be brave."

—ANONYMOUS

The NVA Gets Kate in Its Sights

The deteriorating situation at Kate worsened on the third day when the NVA's numerically superior infantry detachments unleashed a new series of attacks on all of Kate's compass points, this time supported by heavy artillery firing from across the border in Cambodia.

The NVA resumed its attack bright and early on the morning of October 30. Kate reported to II CTZ Mobile Strike Force at 6:20 A.M. that it had received four rounds of 75mm recoilless rifle fire. That was a prelude to a ground attack on the base about half an hour later by a platoon of NVA soldiers wearing khaki uniforms and pith helmets and using small arms and automatic weapons from a distance of about 160 yards. The one artillery gun on the base still capable of working fired back, but with limited effect.

"We used the operable artillery on Kate to direct fire everywhere we could around our defensive perimeter, which had to be checked on a regular basis," Albracht explained. "It was not uncommon to get pinned down by automatic weapons fire when doing so, especially since the NVA could now easily see us."

The day was not off to a good start. It would get worse—far worse—not only for the men on Kate, but for all the friendlies trying to help them. Albracht did all he could to bolster their morale and keep the defenders on their toes, once again setting the example through his tireless leadership.

Keeping his head and still ignoring his wounds, the captain moved back and forth to the most threatening of the attack points, issued sound tactical commands to direct his troops, ordered strikes onto enemy positions that were within mere meters of his own, and exposed himself repeatedly to enemy fire by crossing fire lanes again and again to rescue wounded soldiers, recover the dead, and distribute ammunition and water.

Despite the odds against them, the defenders continued to hold off the NVA assaults. It may not have been particularly reassuring to them even if they had known, but things weren't much better for their counterparts at the other firebases in the area.

A Widespread Attack

Firebases Annie and Martha were also under heavy attack. The situation was getting more and more precarious for the 155th AHC and OPCON pilots. They ignored the danger and continued to fly medevac and supply missions to the bases, always under intense enemy fire.

On the night of October 30, the choppers relocated the personnel on Martha to Duclap to reinforce the camp. Every chopper that came in to remove troops did so under heavy mortar fire. Nevertheless, they managed to move the troops to a new firebase near Duclap, the newly coined LZ Mike Smith, which was named after the officer injured and medevaced from Kate. But every firebase evacuated meant more trouble for Kate because it allowed the NVA to divert more troops there.

Mike Smith could not understand why the firebase was named after him, although he believes the honor was a case of mistaken identity. After he was wounded at Kate and evacuated, Lieutenant Ross replaced him and was killed. Smith returned to Kate on November 1, the last day. Someone got confused and thought that Smith was the man killed there. As a result, the base was named after him. By the time the confusion was sorted out, the name had stuck.

At about 9:30 A.M., at least 500 NVA troops began a sustained ground attack on Kate following the rule that attackers trying to over-run a dug-in enemy need three men for each defender. Enemy .50-caliber and 37mm antiaircraft positions opened up on any aircraft that approached Kate, with devastating effect. Montagnard infantry repulsed the attack, aided by the one piece of artillery and Joker gun-ships and U.S. Air Force F-100 jets dropping 500-pound bombs. They made the difference. The NVA troops could not overrun the base because of those air strikes.

Three gunships and one CH-47 were hit by enemy ground fire in the vicinity of Kate. Two other Joker gunships from the 48th AHC were diverted to Kate. One of them, Joker 85, was shot down and destroyed with the loss of the entire crew while Albracht was directing it. After enemy RPG fire hit the chopper's tail boom, the pilot, Nolan Black, lost control and the helicopter slammed into the ground within sight of the firebase. Black and the others aboard (Maury Hearne, Clyde Canada, and Douglas Lott) were killed.

The loss of Joker 85 was particularly devastating for the troops on Kate, who were concerned over the loss of their comrades trying to protect them. Many of them wondered if their deaths were worth the sacrifice—or if Kate and its defenders were doomed.

Albracht remembers the incident vividly. "At about 0930 hours, we were targeted by a large-scale ground attack from the southwest quadrant of our perimeter," he said. "During this, while directing close gunship support on the NVA attackers, Joker 85 of the 48th Aviation Company was hit and went down in a ball of fire. He was so close I could feel the heat when the bird erupted in fire—a spectacle that still haunts me to this day."

Specialist Fourth Class Nelson Koon recalls the helplessness he felt as Joker 85 went down. Amidst the pounding from rockets and mortars and ground attacks by the enemy, "At one point there were a lot of gunships and Cobras giving us supporting fire." Then Joker 85 was hit. "With the tail boom on fire, I watched as the chopper was going down," Koon said. "I remember yelling, 'Pull it up,' but the chopper crashed in the jungle outside our perimeter. The crew were all dead."

Pierelli had a similar reaction. He described the bodies of the crew members as "one sad sight." The incident brought alive for him the horrors of the war in which he was involved. His concise comment after seeing the crash summed up what many of the troops at Kate were feeing.

"God bless that crew," was all he could say.

CWO1 Harold "Ben" Gay, the commander of the flight, felt the same.

Kate Calls

On October 30, 1969, Gay was the aircraft commander of a UH-1C gunship and the fire team leader for both his gunship and Joker 85. The latter was being flown by CWO2 Black and CWO2 Hearne. The gunners/crew were specialists Canada and Lott. They were flying in support of the Buprang Special Forces compound and Kate. That morning they were directed to help repel a ground attack on the firebase after refueling and rearming at the small dirt strip at Buprang.

The mission began when the aircraft landed at the small refueling strip outside of the barbed wire fence surrounding the Buprang Special Forces compound. The pilots had finished refueling when they started receiving mortar fire from the NVA troops surrounding both Buprang and Kate. The pilots attempted to expedite their takeoffs due to the incoming mortar rounds, but had difficulty getting airborne due to the weight of the aircraft from the fuel they had put on board.

Gay and "Blackie" both made several attempts to take off on the short strip, but each time their main rotor rpms dropped and their transmission oil temperature lights came on, indicating that they were stressing both their engines and transmissions. They received a call over their UHF radios from the FAC indicating that Kate had come under a ground attack by NVA troops. Gay and Black threw caution to the wind.

They made another takeoff run down the short strip. Gay went first. As he came to the end of the strip, he continued, even though the rpm level was dropping again. He was taking a major chance. At the end of the strip there was a slight cliff. Gay ignored it and kept on going. As his aircraft dropped, he was able to build his rpms and keep the chopper in the air. Black and Hearne duplicated the maneuver. They were airborne and headed for Kate.

Where Did All the NVA Come From?

As both aircraft approached Kate at low level from the west, they were below the top of the firebase's hilltop location. As they flew around the firebase, still approximately fifty feet off the ground to the east side of the hill, they observed a huge mass of NVA soldiers coming out of the tree line, heading up the hill, and assaulting the firebase.

Gay and Black opened fire immediately with their rockets. Due to the close range, the rockets' warheads did not travel the required 100 yards to arm and were simply hitting the soldiers. (After the rockets are fired they rotate, and it takes approximately 100 yards for the rotation to place the firing pin in the warhead in a position where it will explode.)

Between the two choppers' door gunners and their mini-guns, they inflicted a number of casualties on the NVA during their first pass. They circled back and began a second pass. That time they were farther away, which provided sufficient room for the rockets to arm. That allowed both aircraft to engage the ground forces again with all their weapons.

By the time Gay and Black completed several passes, they had inflicted severe casualties on the NVA. The pilots had stopped the ground attack, despite the heavy small-arms ground fire their aircraft had received from the attacking force.

Let's Do It Again

Gay and Black flew to another dirt strip outside of the area of Buprang and Kate, where they could rearm. The location also provided a longer dirt strip to take off from. Significantly, this location was not coming under enemy mortar or ground fire.

While rearming, Gay spoke to Black and Hearne about returning and again providing fire support for the besieged firebase. Black agreed. They departed for the short flight back to the area of Kate and the Buprang compound. The Amy O-1 "Birddog" FAC who was on scene was assigning targets and missions to the flights of U.S. Air Force fighter jets and other U.S. Army gunship teams, which were in the area to escort the lift helicopters as they attempted to land troops and supplies at the firebase.

Gay contacted the FAC. This time he assigned Gay's fire team the mission of destroying a suspected NVA antiaircraft (AA) site that reportedly consisted of at least one .51-caliber AA gun. Gay located the area of the AA site and began an attack run. Black and Hearne followed.

After several passes of engaging the weapon, Gay turned in behind Black and observed AA ground fire coming from a second .51-caliber AA site. That fire struck Black's aircraft.

Chopper Down!

Gay witnessed flames coming from the bottom of Black's aircraft in the area of the oil cooler exhaust. He called "Blackie" on the VHF radio and said, "85 (Joker 85), this is 73: you're on fire! Put it down."

Joker 85 responded, and asked, "Where's a field?"

Unfortunately, the area was hilly and mostly covered in heavy jungle vegetation with open fields scattered between the jungle growth. That was the last thing Gay heard from them. He saw their tail boom separate at the point where it attached to the body of the aircraft. The body of the aircraft immediately went inverted at approximately fifty feet above the jungle and exploded upon impact.

Gay circled around the location, but he had to depart due to the heavy enemy ground fire, hits on his aircraft, and his inability to see anything down in the jungle. Other pilots told him over the radio to leave the area lest he, too, succumb to the ground fire. Reluctantly, he began climbing away.

Gay requested another aircraft to fly up and check his aircraft for damage and fluid leaks that may have resulted from the ground fire. He returned to Ninh Hoa and reported the incident to command. As bad as he and the troops on the ground felt about the loss of Joker 85, he had to carry on. He was flying missions again the next day, when the troops at Kate were under even more pressure.

"We're on Our Own"

There were considerable amounts of grief and of speculation among other pilots and crew members about Joker 85's fate. The grief was compounded by the fact that Black and his wife Carol had adopted a baby just before he left for Vietnam. That meant one more child in the U.S. would grow up without a father, which was becoming an all-too-common experience there. The remaining pilots wanted to know what forced Joker 85 down, so they could be prepared for a similar experience.

Pat Ewing remembered vividly the day Joker 85 went down. He wasn't near Kate when the incident occurred. He heard about it over the radio, but he didn't know it was one of 48th AHC's for a while.

"I think we were refueling at Buprang at the time or just getting airborne when we heard chatter that it was one of our ships," Ewing said. "It was later when I found out that Nolan Black, who had roomed with me temporarily, was in the aircraft when it was hit by an RPG and lost its tail boom."

Ewing wondered about the cause. "I've always wondered if it was possible that the ship was hit by a shoulder-fired missile, since it would be a hell of a shot to hit an aircraft going sixty to eighty knots with a single shot, and the fact that a heat-seeking missile would have homed in on the exhaust of the turbine engine, which comes out at that juncture, is puzzling."

Other troops heard later that the pilot and the crew chief may have survived the crash, but were killed by the NVA. Koon thought that being killed by the NVA might be his fate as well. He noticed that after Joker 85 went down all their chopper air support disappeared.

He thought, "Well, isn't that great? Now we are on our own." He was right for the most part.

The incident had a more profound and foreboding impact on Kate, though. It marked the end of helicopter gunship support for the base during daylight hours due to the increasing danger to the crews. The ground fire, coming relentlessly from all directions, made it suicidal for anything other than the fast Air Force fighters to work in close proximity. From that point on, jets would provide the only air support. Despite the dangers, chopper pilots kept flying missions, even though Kate had been, for all practical purposes, cut off.

Chapter 10

Tracers
Can Be Traced

"Brave Cannons."

—MOTTO OF THE 92ND ARTILLERY

A Unique Use for Tracers

After the midmorning assault ended, a CH-47 flying crane dropped in a replacement 105 howitzer. The gun's arrival paid off immediately.

Albracht spotted an enemy artillery piece firing at Kate. He used tracer rounds fired from his M16 to guide the howitzer crew's return fire. His tactic, although highly risky, worked. As Albracht explained, "When I used tracers to direct the FAC's marking rockets into a specific target, as well as directing the Huey gunships, it had never been done before to the best of my knowledge. It was an idea that came to me borne out of frustration at not being able to pinpoint the FAC's rockets and the gunships' fire, therefore the actual air strike."

The artillery gunners landed a direct hit on the enemy gun, causing some secondary explosions, indicating that they might have hit a small ammo or fuel dump as well.

Using tracers as marking rounds was effective, but extremely dangerous. Enemy personnel could locate the person firing them simply by eyeballing their origin. But the troops at Kate had no choice. They had to let air support providers know where their targets were. Jets spent the day dropping napalm and 500-pound bombs to keep the NVA at bay—but not completely. Then again, the NVA could not completely keep U.S. helicopters away from Kate. Conversely, they seemed determined to invite their presence.

At noon, defenders at Kate spotted about twenty NVA soldiers within 100 meters northeast of the base. The NVA fired at the "friend-lies" from the tree line. Then a group of NVA soldiers, estimated at company size, attacked Kate. This group, wearing gray uniforms and pith helmets and armed with automatic weapons and assorted small arms, launched a quick attack, which ended almost as soon as it started. They broke contact within a couple minutes and withdrew north.

TAC called in fire on the retreating NVA troops, with unknown results (which was usually the case). There were no friendly casualties in the attack. The brief assault showed that the NVA were getting closer, growing bolder, and increasing in numbers, as confirmed by an S-2 report on October 30.

According to the report, 600 NVA troops were sighted about seven miles west of Duclap, moving east. S-2 speculated that they belonged to the K394 NVA Artillery-Infantry Battalion—the same unit identified in the documents captured on October 28. The situa-tion at Kate in particular, and the region in general, concerned Albracht, everyone for whom he was responsible, and the air support personnel assigned to protect them.

Hold Your Water

The Montagnards rushed for the water trailer. Albracht recognized at once that they were more concerned with survival than discipline. That was the last thing he needed. If they had any chance at all of surviving, they had to maintain battlefield discipline. Wisely, he stepped in, held the Montagnards in check, and ordered them to go for water one man at a time. Then he allowed the artillerymen to get their water. Disci-pline was restored, at least for the moment.

The day dragged on without any major incidents until about 6 P.M. Lieutenant John Kerr had spent most of the day calling in 155 howitzer fire from Firebase Susan, where Captain Adam and Lieutenant Bamford were located with two of his battery's other guns. The distance made supporting fire tricky and created almost as much danger for the Kate contingent as the enemy's guns did. The one difference was that Kerr, Adam, and Bamford could at least control their own guns.

Kate was at maximum range from Susan, eight to nine miles away. So it was tricky for the gunners on Susan to get rounds to land close enough to Kate to help the troops there. They tried anyway, but they lost their FDC man on Kate.

At 6 P.M., while Kerr was adjusting this artillery from Susan, enemy shrapnel embedded itself in his left thigh. Despite the injury (which bothers him to this day), he dragged himself around on one leg, adjusting artillery until dark. The defenders needed it, especially around 7 P.M., when the NVA launched a massive attack that was held back by jets and Spooky crews who had been warned that the attack was imminent.

Here They Come Again

"At about 1900 hours, I moved to an open position on our perimeter after receiving word that the NVA were massing in the woodline at the northeast end of Kate," Albracht reported. That put him in a precarious spot once again. "I had to be in the open to observe the entire attack so I could effectively direct both the air support and the Kate ground defenders."

The massive NVA ground attack began almost immediately, with well over 500 NVAers pouring out of the surrounding jungle. Albracht directed the sorties of Air Force F-100s dropping 500-pound bombs. The defenders repelled the attack, but not before the enemy penetrated their perimeter. Luckily for the friendlies, a Shadow had come on station earlier at dusk, and it helped repel the attack. Later that evening, Spooky also came on station. Albracht worked both of them all night and up to first light.

One of the casualties of the evening attack was Lt. Mike Smith, who was wounded and evacuated to Ban Me Thuot for treatment. That was a setback for the artillerymen, who nonetheless decided to step up their part of the battle. As for Smith, he would be back three days later—just in time to escape again.

The artillerymen felt that up until this time their weapons had been underutilized. There was no question that the soldiers were, as their motto suggested, "brave cannons." Brave but underutilized. They decided to exercise some initiative.

The artillerymen informed Albracht and Pierelli that they would start developing their own harassment-and-interdiction (H&I) targets and begin firing more for the defenders' preservation. (H&I missions involve firing on known enemy trails, hangouts, and other similar targets at random times to keep the enemy off balance.) The two security commanders did not object. After all, their survival depended on the artillery too.

The Importance of H&I

Harassment and interdiction may have played a major role in the outcome of the battle for Kate. To this day, Pierelli believes that the lack of it may have allowed the NVA get so close, dig in, and launch their attacks so successfully. He recalls one morning when he and Albracht, in the same bunker at the time, were awakened by loud, explosive noises.

"I remember him asking me what that was, and I responded that it was the artillery firing," Pierelli explains. "Within seconds, one of the artillery men came running into our bunker yelling '*Duy Uy* [Captain], I'm hit!'"

Pierelli looked at the soldier. Sure enough, there was blood on the back of his uniform.

"We're taking incoming," Pierelli announced.

After the shelling stopped, everyone went into the action mode: wind-sprinting to positions, assessing the wounded, and calling in the medevacs and gunships. That's when the significance of the lack of H&I sunk in for Pierelli, and peace no longer reigned in the valley.

"I remember when I got to Kate, none of the guns were firing harassment and interdiction fire," he says. "Some of the artillery enlisted were complaining because the higher-ups would not allow it." In fact, "it wasn't until we were under attack that those guns were fired while I was there. Under the circumstances, those artillerymen did an outstanding job."

A Damaging Shot in the Arm

During the night, one of the artillerymen accidentally shot another gun crew member, Sergeant Houghtaling, in the arm. Houghtaling, who had bonded with Pierelli, wanted the sergeant to treat him. Pierelli knelt near the wounded artilleryman and tried to comfort him. It was obvious to Pierelli that Houghtaling was in pain.

The artillery medic had already administered first aid and morphine. Pierelli noticed that the morphine was not helping. He instructed the medic to give the wounded soldier a bit more, then marked the wounded man's forehead with an "M" to indicate that morphine had been administered. Then he called for a Dustoff to evacuate him.

"The medevac came in on a night of heavy fog," Pierelli remembers. "The pilot did a remarkable job." The chopper took Houghtaling and Kerr to the 71st Evac Hospital in Pleiku. From there, Kerr went to the 6th Convalescent Hospital in Cam Ranh Bay, where he spent six weeks before going back to his unit to finish his year of duty.

The incident demonstrated two factors at play at Kate. First, the troops were placing an inordinate amount of faith in Pierelli. And, miraculously, choppers were still flying in and out of Kate—or at least trying to.

Chopper Pilots Left in the Dark

Warrant Officer 1 John "Les" Davison, assigned to the 155th AHC, led a team of two CH-47 Chinooks into Kate that day. The first one got in and out all right while the second took several hits on its approach. His ship was hit by enemy gunfire as well. Nevertheless, he was right back at Kate the following night, despite the dangers.

Davison emphasized the conditions chopper pilots faced at that time:

> A night mission, as flown by the 155th to resupply LZ Kate, was very unusual. In fact, it was the only company-sized operation conducted during total darkness during my tour.
>
> We had no night vision equipment, no GPS, no radar altimeters, nor were Navaids available. We used FM radio homing to fly to the area, located the LZ by sighting a strobe light, and approached and hovered to the strobe to drop the ammo. In plain English, the helicopters and crews were at considerable risk in conducting this mission, but the risks were considered acceptable because the situation at LZ Kate was so desperate.

Desperate it was. That only made the troops more determined to do their jobs and increase their chances of survival. Midnight of October 30 arrived: they had survived another day. Halloween was fast upon them. The trick was to stay alive at least one more day, despite the mounting odds against them. The NVA determined to treat them to attacks on October 31 worse than any they had unleashed up until then. That is exactly what they did.

Day 5

October 31, 1969

Chapter 11

Trick or Treat

"Happy Halloween. The Spookys are out."

—SPOOKY 41 TO CHICKENHAWK

If Nothing Else, the NVA Were Predictable

At first light, the incoming volume increased dramatically. That was followed by yet another ground attack, but Kate's defenders thwarted it. The attack was not a surprise. In fact, it was predictable: between midnight and dawn, troops at Kate had seen flashlights in the enemy positions. Albracht and Pierelli, who were constantly moving about the perimeter, checking defenses, and trying to observe enemy movement, saw them too.

The 105 crew members were pretty sure it wasn't NVA soldiers reading under their blankets, so they fired directly on the positions. The defenders also heard sounds of digging and troop movement in the NVA area all night, especially at the south end of Kate.

Albracht asked Spooky and Shadow to saturate the area with gunfire. The artillery fire and air cover from the two planes did not deter the NVA soldiers from carrying out their appointed rounds, however.

The jets continued to work the area, but after every airstrike the base would be shelled again as if the NVA were saying "We're still here."

The Two Worst Times of Day

First light and dusk were the two most vulnerable times for Kate's defenders. Spooky and Shadow were usually gone at dawn because their slow speeds made them easy targets in daylight, and there was not enough light at either time for fighters and choppers to fly. So Kate always got hit hard at first light.

Albracht was a fast learner. This was his fourth day on the base. Knowing that the NVA would attack as usual, he requested Spooky or Shadow to remain on station until the FAC could start bringing in the TAC air. Without Spooky's and Shadow's willing extensions in the morning and early arrivals in the evening, the defenders would not have been able to repel the ground attacks. Even with their help it was getting harder and harder to fight off the NVA.

Beyond a "Tracer" of Doubt

Albracht used his newly developed technique of using tracer ammunition to direct the FAC precisely. He would go to a point in the perimeter and lay down a steady stream of tracer fire from his M16 to the exact enemy position that he wanted hit by air cover elements. The FAC used the tracer stream to aim a marking rocket at the impact location, then the fast-moving jets would roll in and bomb on the marker.

The first time Albracht used that strategy there was no response from the NVA. But they quickly figured out what he was doing and made him a marked man every time he employed the tracer technique after that. That was a major drawback as far as Albracht was concerned.

His approach required him to be in the open when firing. He really did not have any other choice. The captain felt that the benefits of pinpoint bombing outweighed his personal risk. Besides, the presence of air support was reassuring to Kate's defenders. It was important to them that they knew they were not abandoned, as the 23rd ARVN Division seemed to have done when it refused to provide any reinforcements.

This apparent abandonment began to demoralize the Montagnards, who discussed leaving Kate, which the NVA was hitting from 360 degrees. There were constant artillery battles, with the howitzers firing both direct and indirect fire. Both 155mm howitzers had been knocked out by this time, and the 105mm howitzer could only fire at a limited elevation. The artillerymen were now being used mostly as infantry. Chaos reigned and bombs rained as the day wore on and more troops aboard Kate were hit.

Injuries Start to Take Their Toll

At 10:15 A.M., a 57mm recoilless rifle round from the northwest wounded three friendly soldiers, one of them seriously, and killed one. Fifteen minutes later, a B-40 rocket from the east seriously wounded another defender. Then, at 11:20 A.M., several NVA 82mm mortar rounds believed to have been fired from the east landed on the base. One defender was wounded seriously in that attack. At about the same time, another incoming 57mm recoilless rifle round killed an artilleryman. The attacks continued.

Around 12:20 P.M., five B-40 rockets hit in the general vicinity of the base. Three exploded in the perimeter. They killed another artilleryman and wounded one more. The stress was getting to the artillerymen, as two more were medevaced out due to "shock," commonly called battle fatigue. As Albracht explained, "The constant combat and incoming artillery just plain wore us down. Some soldiers cracked under the pressure. It is a fact of life that some people are stronger than others—period."

In the space of two hours, NVA fire had killed, wounded, or forced out of action thirteen defenders. Kate could not sustain that rate of losses for long—and the fact that the NVA rounds were coming from different directions suggested that enemy troops were building a ring around the base.

A crewmember cleans a 155mm howitzer at LZ Kate.

A 105mm howitzer crew ready for action at LZ Kate.

Reg Brockwell leans on a 105mm howitzer.
Note the 8-inch howitzer barrel elevated in the background.

A 155mm. howitzer emplacement at ¯Z Kate.

Reg Brockwell (left) and 105mm howitzer crewmembers at LZ Kate.

The crew of a 105mm howitzer demonstrate the loading process.

Sgt. Gerald V. "Tex" Rogers behind a machine gun.

Troops at rest at LZ Kate.

"Tex" Rogers carries fresh food for LZ Kate troops.

"Tex" Rogers prepares meat for the troops.

From left to right: Dwight Willingham, Rod Lewis, and Paul Gilbert—all advisors to Montagnard troops—and Reg Brockwell.

A 105mm howitzer crew at LZ Kate.

Bath day at a Montagnard village near LZ Kate.

Lt. Col. Elton Delaune (left) and unidentified soldiers gather.

From left to right: Major Walker, an unknown soldier, Lieutenant Colonel Delaune, District Chief Major No, and MACV advisor Captain Parker confer.

How many people can fit on an army 6 x 6 truck?

USAF Capt. Al Dykes, a.k.a. Spooky 41.

Spooky Headquarters.

Crewmembers aboard Spooky man their guns.

The Spooky logo on the nose of an aircraft.

A crewmember checks machine guns aboard Spooky.

We Need Guns—and Everything Else

Certainly, the folks back at II CTZ Mobile Strike Force HQ were aware of Kate's situation and were working hard to alleviate the pressure on it. At 10:30 A.M., they had noted that not only was Kate under rocket attack, but the defenders needed guns. Sadly, the guns and a hook (CH-47) to transport them had been requested the previous day, but they had not materialized. At 10:50 A.M., HQ recorded that they were finally underway.

The next problem was ammunition. At 10:55 A.M., Captain Nichola advised Captain Twiggs and Captain Ramey that Kate's ammo status was critical. That set off the usual round of radio calls and red tape. Colonel Hawthorn visited HQ to discuss the ammo situation, and Captain Gresham called back regarding the issue.

Major Burr and Colonel Hawthorn discussed the hook and decided to divert one that had been moving troops to Buprang. It would transport ammo to Kate instead. While all this was going on, the defenders at Kate waited for relief. They waited a long time. Entry after entry in the II CTZ Mobile Strike Force–Kate logs show that there was a great deal of prioritizing going on, but little action to see that supplies were delivered to Kate.

While the supplies were on the line, so were the lives of the dwindling number of combat-ready troops at Kate. At 2:30 P.M., fifteen rounds of B-40 rocket fire from the northeast headed toward the base. Six of them impacted on the south side of the perimeter. They did not wound any of the defenders.

Twenty minutes later, the base received six rounds of 82mm mortar fire and four B-40 rockets. They were fired from the southeast, east, north, and west. This time, one defender was killed. The noose was tightening, and the need for supplies was growing more critical.

At 4:45 P.M., the ammo had still not arrived at Kate. It had been loaded aboard aircraft that departed the HQ area at 2 P.M., but they took the ammo to Buprang instead of Kate. That was of no use to Albracht and his troops, who were receiving B-40 and mortar rounds from NVA gunners at fifteen-minute intervals.

An entry in the HQ log indicated that "Enemy weapons were well zeroed into friendly positions." It didn't take a log entry for Albracht to recognize that he and his troops were on the receiving end of it, and the enemy's rounds were raising havoc with them.

Smith Departs—and Returns

At one point during an attack that day, Lieutenant Smith took shrapnel in his face and nose area, and had to be medevaced out quickly. Anyone with a modicum of sense—and a choice—would have stayed away. Smith had the choice, but not the sense. Albracht noted that the very next day, "I was more than a little surprised to see him returning on an inbound medevac with his wounds cleaned and his nose bandaged. He now had an appropriate radio call sign that he had truly earned—'Beak.'"

Smith earned everyone's respect when he arrived back at Kate. "This showed again the incredible caliber of the men I was with at Kate," Albracht stressed. "Smith could have stayed in the rear and no one would have ever said a word. But he felt duty-bound to be with his men. He was not just *a* leader, but *their* leader. He was with them in the beginning and he would be with them at the end. He was an outstanding asset to Sergeant Pierelli and me in the overall defense of Kate."

There was one other personnel change of note that day. Lieutenant Maurice Zollner arrived to replace Lieutenant Kerr. He, too, arrived just in time to walk out the next night.

It's a Long Shot from Buprang to Kate

Troubles kept mounting for the troops at Kate. They were still low on ammo, which remained at Buprang. At 4:55 P.M., Captain Twiggs told HQ that "Hook 01 at Buprang is scheduled to take in ammo right after arc light strikes, going in now." It took the B-52s a while to reach Kate, apparently.

Requests and updates at Buprang revealed that the ammo was not getting any closer to Kate. Ominously, an update at 5:45 P.M. reported: "The FSB Kate CO stated that ammo must arrive sunset of that day or the FSB would be overrun. CPT Portman contacted LTC Veazey, S4, and Major Mejia, Deputy S4. Major Long stated that a convoy to

BAN ME THUOT may take ammo. It did not." A follow-up at 7:30 P.M.: "Major Doglione, Air Force liaison to the 5th SFGA, advised against airdrop at night on such a small target. CPT Portman advised that emergency request for ammo could be submitted to the ARVN ammo depot (Class B) through the 5th ALCMACV Advisor."

Meanwhile, Back at the Ranch . . .

Night fell once again at Kate. Albracht could still hear the NVA digging. This time they were closer. He called in Spooky and Shadow, but the digging continued. Moreover, Spooky preferred to delay immediate support so it wouldn't expend its ammunition and fuel and have to leave the base prematurely. The fact that they were on station was somewhat reassuring, as the conversation between the Spooky's navigator, Al Dykes, known also as the "Alabama Boy," and Albracht indicated:

> **CH:** I'll be putting out a strobe for you, a strobe, right on our firebase here. We've only got one, and it's low on batteries, so I'm going to put it in and let's get a real good adjustment and then I gotta turn it off. Is this OK with you?

> **41:** Roger that and Chickenhawk Outlaw 25 said that he'd kind of like us to just fly around a little bit before we start expending or dropping too many flares so we can extend our time with you, over.

> **CH:** That's a roger roger roger on that buddy. Like I was telling the 61, I've worked him before, real good people there, and as long as they hear you up there, you put out a little bit here and a little bit there, they're not going to try a hell of a lot because they know what you people can do, they know you can shoot up every time they move with you people up there.

> **41:** Roger that and, by the way Chickenhawk, Happy Halloween, the Spookys are out.

Finally, at 5:45 P.M., A-236 reported that a resupply chopper was going into Kate. The pilot had received a red light indicator warning of danger, so he dropped the ammo he was carrying on the south slope of the firebase hill. The rest of the entry was chilling: "Ammo can not be recovered, trying to blow in place." That did not help Kate's defenders. Besides, there was plenty of other stuff blowing up around the base— and the news about ammo kept getting worse.

At 6:10 P.M., Major Tennis of LSC advised HQ that two C-130 aircraft with ammo were en route to Ban Me Thuot with an estimated time of arrival of 7:05 P.M. LSC had already turned the ammo over to IFFV for transport. That was the good news. The bad news came twenty-five minutes later, when Tennis said that the airdrop could not be accomplished that night.

As things turned out, it would not have made a difference if the airdrop had been approved. Major Burr said that he could not make choppers available from either A-235 or A-236 that night.

To no one's surprise, Kate was still under fire. At 9 P.M., HQ received a request from the base for Shadow—and ammo. It was clear that Albracht's situation was getting worse by the minute. The wrangling over what ammo could be dropped at Kate, who was going to make the attempt, and when, continued at HQ. The final decision was clear: the mission could not be completed until first light on November 1. At least there was ammo available.

The process may have been slow, but various elements in the area were contributing what they could to resupply the base. The ARVN donated carbine ammo. IFFV furnished ammo for the Browning automatic rifles (BARs). The choppers to make the drop were assembled and delivery was scheduled for the next morning. The only hope was that the troops would still be at Kate when it arrived.

Plan B

Albracht resigned himself to the fact that the defenders would have to fend for themselves that evening. He called for an Arc Light strike. Shortly thereafter, he received a message to take extreme cover. At 10:10 P.M., the B-52s responded.

The planes dropped one-ton bombs in a "Danger Close" operation, in which the bombs hit so close to Kate that the defenders actually sustained some casualties. As Albracht explained, "It had to be done, though, and the strike brought us some much-needed time after being nearly overrun." Unfortunately, they did not buy any time for artillery Lt. Ronald Alan Ross.

According to U.S. military spokesmen, two missions of three to twelve bombers each dropped their thirty-ton loads on suspected NVA concentrations along the Cambodian border in Quangduc Province. The strike granted the defenders a short reprieve, but as soon as the B-52s left, the NVA resumed its shelling.

During the shelling, Albracht and Ross talked in a small bunker. The two men had just met. Ross was a happy man at that point. He had just learned that he had become a father of a son named John Anthony. "That was actually the first day I had a chance to talk to him," Albracht recalled. "We were in a rather small bunker and talking about the very bad situation we were in. But we didn't want to dwell on that too much, so we shifted into personal topics. For example, we asked each other where we were from 'back in the world,' as we referred to home." Ross revealed that he was from Wisconsin and Albracht that he was from neighboring Illinois. Ross mentioned his newborn son, whom he hoped to see when he went on R&R.

Eventually, Albracht told Ross he that he needed to run to the command bunker. The captain advised Ross to wait until he reached the bunker before he moved, after which Albracht left. "I lit out and saw the B-40 rocket launch and the tail heading toward us," he recounted. "Ross was a few meters behind. When the round hit, it threw me into the bunker. I wasn't hurt, but a piece of B-40 shrapnel lodged itself in the lieutenant's neck. He collapsed into my arms."

Albracht tried to stop the blood, but it spewed unabated. Ross bled out right there in Albracht's arms.

By the time Ross was killed, all of the troops—the Yards and the U.S. troops alike—were strained to the limit. Some of them were literally immobile from the stress. Two U.S. soldiers broke down and had to be medevaced. The pounding Kate was receiving was relentless; it never stopped completely for more than twenty or thirty minutes. Yet Albracht did not stop looking for ways to protect the base and his troops.

The captain spent his days directing TAC air from all points of Kate's perimeter and his nights directing Shadow and Spooky. Hardly anyone was getting any sleep. Albracht was getting about two hours of sleep a night, sometimes three. The 155s were knocked out, the 105 was crippled, and it was practically suicidal to be in the parapet to man the guns. The NVA had the entire firebase zeroed in.

Chapter 12

The Cavalry Arrives

*"When our guys are getting shot at and ask for help,
you don't pay much attention to the weather. You just get your
butt out there as fast as possible, no matter what."*

—STAN GAUSE, 134TH AHC BASED OUT OF PHU HIEP

At last, relief arrived. At about 2 A.M. on November 1, Kate received an emergency resupply of ammunition and medical supplies from the 155th Aviation Company. Four resupply slicks and five gunships arrived at the base. This resupply was absolutely critical, because the defenders were almost completely out of everything.

The slicks brought in almost enough to repel a sustained large-scale ground attack—almost. As the troopers broke down the ammo and medical supplies for distribution, Albracht noticed that body bags were included and the number was not small. Albracht was sure they were sent with the best of intentions, but they brought home the realities of an increasingly desperate situation.

The Resupply Story

John "Les" Davison describes the resupply mission:

On the night of 31 Oct/l Nov, I led a flight of four UH-l C gunships escorting five 155th ABC slicks on an emergency night resupply mission into LZ Kate. I have no direct knowledge of events on the ground at or near LZ Kate, but the following may be pertinent.

I fought hard against going on the mission. We had flown all day, and had taken a lot of fire, and some hits. When we finally recovered at Ban Me Thuot well after nightfall, the whole team was exhausted. It took me a while to wind down from the tensions of the day's combat; once I did, I was out. But the intruder finally roused me into consciousness. "Emergency resupply mission. The CO is briefing in Operations in ten minutes."

In the darkness outside, several other Falcon and Stagecoach pilots were making their way to the 155 Assault Helicopter Company Operations hooch. As we entered, the clock showed 0010 hours; the CO and platoon leaders were poring over tactical maps, the Ops officer was on the field phone. All had obviously been busy since the mission alert first came down. The eyes of the pilots in the audience were mostly bloodshot—and a little scared. We had an idea what was coming.

After all were present, Major Owen himself led the briefing. LZ Kate, one of the artillery firebases recently established to support the Special Forces border camp at Buprang, had itself come under heavy attack during the preceding two days.

All of us had flown into or near Kate during the fighting, so were already familiar with the tactical situation. Just a few hours earlier, I had led a Falcon team to escort two Freight Train Chinooks into Kate. When we arrived, two Undertaker Cobras happened to be on station, and together we covered the first CH-47 in and out without incident. But that expended the Snakes, and our two Charlies just couldn't put out enough firepower to cover the second Hook as well. He made it out OK—but not without taking several hits. The area was definitely HOT!

The firebase was holding out, but the defenders were low on ammunition and weren't sure they could wait until first light for resupply. We were tasked to deliver four slick loads of M-16, carbine, and M-60 ammo. Mission planning called for five slicks and four guns. If we weren't alert before, we certainly were now. I'd never been on a mission where we took an empty rescue ship. GULP!

The best, most experienced pilots had been picked to fly this one; two senior aircraft commanders in each slick. Credit to Major Owen, though. He knew it was a tough mission, but he didn't just send others out to accomplish it. He would be co-pilot in the lead ship—right where a good CO should be (but where many COs weren't).

Our briefing covered the weather, enemy situation, frequencies, and formations. Then Major Owen looked to me (gunship lead) and asked, "Are the Falcons going to go in hot?"

Pete Cosmos, a brand-new aircraft commander, but never at a loss for words, responded immediately. "Damn straight we will!" he exclaimed. But the major still looked to me.

I've often wondered whether Pete's outburst affected my response, and I just don't know the answer. In any case, my reply was a different one.

"I'd rather wait to see if Charlie will let us do it without shooting. We'll be on both sides of you, ready to bring smoke—and if they do start up, we can pinpoint the source and be right on it. But you slick guys are the ones hanging out; we'll do whatever you want."

Major Owen didn't hesitate.

"Okay, we'll go in cold unless Chuck starts something. They're still loading the birds. Start time will be 0110; crank on me. Good luck."

Everybody got their gear and headed to the ships, to find the crews already there. After making sure everything was set, most of us wandered back to the platoon hooches for coffee, smokes, a few quick hands of poker, and probably a letter or two home. Even the pilots who weren't flying joined in, and the Dustoff guys, too. As they say, you could have cut the tension with a knife.

Even though it was still too early, the Falcon card game broke up and we headed slowly toward the revetments. The slick pilots were doing the same. Though there were quite a few flight crew and others around, it was unusually quiet. We all knew this one was different. We rechecked the ships again—and then waited. There was little of the usual happy-go-lucky banter between and among the crews; instead, there was lots of nervous chatter and forced laughter. Time dragged.

Finally, it was 0110. We had been strapped in for a good five minutes listening for the telltale whine of the CO's ship starting up, but only heard silence. 0115; more nervous chatter, but no crank. What's the problem?

It was nearly 0130 when we finally cranked. We all got off OK, and the flight out to Kate was uneventful, except for the damn lump in my throat. One of our Peter Pilots made a tape recording of the mission, and during the flight out Falcon 4 (Denny Fenlon) quite clearly told me he was moving his team to the slicks' right side, but I had to ask him to repeat it three times before I could understand. Even my ears were scared!

And then, as we neared the LZ, any hope for surprise (like a flight of nine Hueys at altitude on a quiet, clear night can surprise anybody?) was lost when we couldn't pick up Kate's strobe light and had to make a 360-degree orbit over the area.

"Hey Chuck, are you awake!"

The lump in my throat just kept getting bigger and bigger.

When Stagecoach 6 turned inbound, our two Falcon gun teams rolled out to follow him in, one team on each side. High above, Chalk 5 vectored us to the strobe that marked LZ Kate. Down into the darkness we went; all eyes were on Stagecoach Lead. At 500 meters, Jim began to slow the helicopter. Over the firebase, he came to a hover for a few seconds – just long enough for the ammo boxes to be pushed out. Then we heard, "6 is coming out." OK!

But were the bad guys just setting up for Chalk 2? 2 was in right behind Lead, and he made it OK, and 3 was in. And 4 was in closely behind, and then out again. To everyone's relief, the drop went off without a hitch. I'd never admit it to them, but those Stagecoach guys had big kahunas!

The ammo was delivered, and not a round was fired.

THANK YOU CHUCK!

The slicks climbed out and joined up as they headed east to Ban Me Thuot. Our Falcon teams followed, somewhat more slowly. The ground guys poured out their thanks to Stagecoach 6. The group commander, Eagle 6, pronounced, "Well done" from approximately 50,000-plus feet. The radio chatter was noticeably livelier as we headed back.

Is Spooky 41 Right?

There was one consolation for Albracht. As the siege continued, he, Spooky 41 (Al Dykes), and "Beak" (Lt. Mike Smith) were all on the radio together for long periods of time. "Four-one" was a reassuring voice in what was fast becoming a desperate situation. But in Buprang and Ban Me Thuot, the outlook was becoming bleaker.

Although Dykes assured everyone aboard Kate that they would make it through this battle, Albracht had an uneasy feeling that he didn't really believe it, but he kept that opinion to himself.

Chapter 13

Puff, the
Magic Dragon

*"The VC also knew of 'Puff.' Captured documents often referred to
the plane and said not to attack the 'dragon' since weapons were
useless against it and would only infuriate the monster."*

—LAWRENCE M. GREENBERG*

It is a safe bet that Kate would not have lasted as long as it did if the
Spooky and Shadow airplanes were not overhead. That was the case
throughout Vietnam. Allied ground troops were always happy to have
Spooky and Shadow in the skies above them. Enemy troops did not
share their enthusiasm.

Because of its impressive firepower, the allied troops nicknamed
Spooky "Puff, the Magic Dragon." They may not have known the
pilots or the crews, but they paid them silent thanks for their support
on more than one occasion.

Albracht and one Spooky crew member in particular, navigator Al
Dykes, whose handle was Spooky 41, developed a close relationship in
the few days they worked together at Kate. Later, Dykes said: "I supported a couple of hundred targets, helping the ground troops during
my tour. But Kate is the one I remember most. This I'm sure is because

---

* "'Spooky' Gunship Operations in the Vietnam War," *Vietnam* (April 1990).

106

I felt so close to Hawk and the boys the first time over target. I would have flown every night the rest of my tour in support of Hawk if he had needed a gunship. For some reason I felt part of their struggle."

Spooky 41's Favorite Bird: A Hawk

Ironically, Dykes's favorite bird was a hawk, and it had been long before he got to Vietnam. He acknowledged that "My favorite bird has been the hawk since I was nine years old." In fact, he said, "A couple years back I had my wife paint me a picture of a red-tailed hawk. Maybe that's why I felt like I knew 'Hawk' from the first time we talked on the radio." Whatever the reason, the man on the ground and the man in the sky got to know each other quite well in the short time they worked with one another.

Dykes kept a record of the support he and his crew provided for the complement at Kate. As best as he could determine, his crew dropped more than ninety flares and shot more than 86,000 rounds of lethal 7.62 ammunition on the nights they spent there, which was about four missions' worth. One Spooky started out each flight with 24,000 rounds of ammunition and a large number of flares, which the crew dropped to light up the battleground when necessary.

No Wonder the Enemy Did Not Like Spooky and Shadow

A Spooky was a formidable plane. It was a United States Air Force C-47 Skytrain that had been modified to allow the pilot and crew to fire three 7.62mm General Electric mini-guns through two rear window openings and the side cargo door on the left side of the aircraft, which was the pilot's side.

Each gun could shoot 6,000 rounds per minute on fast fire, and 3,000 on slow fire. Every sixth round was a tracer so the crew could see the rounds hit the ground and walk in their fire if needed. "When we fired it was a constant stream of tracers," Dykes noted.

The pilot had a control on his yoke from which he could control the guns either individually or together. The pilot was not the only person aboard who could activate the guns. The crew included gunners who helped with gun failures and other problems that arose with the weapons.

Spooky's primary function in Vietnam was to provide close air support for allied ground troops. In action, it could fly over a target for hours while providing suppressing fire, usually over an oval-shaped area approximately 52 yards in diameter. The gunners could place a projectile within every 2.4 yards of that oval during a three-second burst. That capability caused enemy troops to be a bit careful when Spooky and Shadow were around.

Explaining the Process

Dykes explained the firing process to Albracht later:

"The pilot has the gun sight up on the left hand side of the aircraft there in his window. Back where I sit on the left hand side I've got a little window that's about 12 inches long and 3 inches wide. And we have got through practice and all to where we put a grease (pencil) mark on our window at the navigator's position, from where we can direct the pilot in to 25 meters (27 yards) of where the bullets are going to hit— using just that little grease mark.

All the communications, as you could probably tell, is handled through the navigator section, and we can't fire until the navigator and the pilot agree on the target. And that's when you heard me saying a couple of times in there "You're clear" or "Look good." He's put the pipper, as we call it, on the target and I agree with him, then he can go ahead and shoot. So that gives you a little bit better rundown on what's happening.

Also, things can get a little hectic as you probably saw in a couple places at Kate. We had about 4 or 5 radios that we monitored simultaneously and on which we listened and talked. So, things got a little tight at times.

The Psychological Edge

The relationship between Dykes and Albracht provided the captain with a major benefit. The ongoing conversations buoyed his spirits and kept him in touch with the outside world, which Albracht wasn't always sure that he was going to see again. But Dykes would not let him feel sorry for himself or lose faith in his mission or his ability to command.

He used humor to take Albracht's mind off his situation and tried to look on the bright side of Kate. That was positive reinforcement for Albracht as he grappled with a situation in which he was not going to get any reinforcements and there was very little of a positive nature to help his spirits.

The Conversation

In the back-and-forth that follows, "Chickenhawk" refers to Albracht (CH); Spooky 41 Victor is Dykes (41).

CH: About how far are you from my location?

41: We're about 15 minutes out, over.

CH: I'll be putting out a strobe for you, a strobe, right on our firebase here. We've only got one, and it's low on batteries, so I'm going to put it in and let's get a real good adjustment and then I gotta turn it off. . . . Like I was telling the 61, I've worked him before, real good people there. As long as they hear you up there, you put out a little bit here and a little bit there, they're not going to try a hell of a lot because they know what you people can do. They know you can shoot up every time they move with you people up there. Listen, have I ever worked you before?

41: I was over here the other night, buddy.

CH: OK, real fine, real fine, I'm glad you're familiar with the area. Give you a little update, this is . . . has been heaviest yet, we took all kinds of shit today. I ain't kidding you, every time we turned around we were getting it. So, that's why, when I'm directing you all around the perimeter, believe me it's all there.

41: Roger, buddy, and I got a question to ask you. Is your position on top of a scraped-off hill with about 50 meters from your position a tree line starts and just north of your position another bald hill with a clump of trees right in the center of it?

CH: That's us, baby. You been here before.

41: Roger, I know where you're at.

CH: To our northwest we have friendlies, so I won't be working you too much in that area, not maybe over 2,200 meters out, over.

41: Roger, how far out from your northwest are the friendlies?

CH: No sweat on that, buddy. I don't want to put that kind of information out, but no problem there, I got a real good safe distance in between them.

41: Ok, we'll be staying with you

CH: Unjust Chaser, Unjust Chaser, Unjust Chaser, this is Chickenhawk, over.

Unjust Chaser: Chickenhawk, Chickenhawk, Unjust Chaser, Unjust Chaser.

41: Outlaw 25, are you calling Spooky 41?

Carbon Outlaw 25: Negative on that, sir, someone was calling 25. Go ahead, this is 25.

CH: Mine's on the way [referring to a Spooky].

Shadow 61: Roger, 25, this is Shadow 61. You ready to copy mission report?

Carbon Outlaw 25: Roger . . .

Unjust Chaser: OK, this is Unjust Chaser, we requested 'em, when we get 'em, they'll be right out to you . . .

CH: Okay, I guess I can't ask for anything more. Thank you much, then. And I'll be waiting for them. And I sure you got them in, get them in here tomorrow. I'll need them tomorrow night.

Unjust Chaser: Roger, Unjust Chaser will be standing by.

41: Just direct us in. We'll save all the light we can, yours and ours.

CH: Okay, buddy. I'm going put on my strobe here in about Zero Two.

41: OK, we'll be looking for it. (Internal: Okay, the guy on the ground is going to put his strobe up in about 1 minute 30 seconds so be looking right off our nose. I'll try to roll in so we can see it.)

41: Hawk, Spooky 41. You Firebase Kate?

CH: That's affirmative.

41: OK, Juliet wants to know if resupply has been accomplished. What's going on so far?

CH: Hey Spook, do you know who the Juliet character is?

41: I don't. Juliet, can you identify yourself?

Juliet: Bravo Mike Tango Division Control, over.

41: Roger, Juliet, copy. Kate, that's Bravo Mike Tango Division Control.

CH: On the resupply status we got in everything they sent us today, except the one. It cut loose and it's setting in the wood line right now.

41: And what was that?

CH: That was the last one. I'm pretty sure it was from Unjust Chaser's location.

41 (to Juliet): He relays that they got them all except the last one and it was cut loose and it's in the woods somewhere. Over.

Juliet: Roger, thank you very much. Out.

CH (to 41): Thanks a lot, buddy. Hey, listen I'm going to go down, but I'll be monitoring you here. So, if it takes me a couple of minutes to get back to you, no sweat.

41: Okay. We'll probably be hanging about another ten minutes before we get ready to start shooting. I just talked to Carbon Outlaw 25 and he advises I am clear to work with you. (Internal: Man, how would you like to be stationed out here? It's a bitch about not having any water half the day. Sure as hell wouldn't get bored though.)

CH: It's getting a little nippy down here, so, I'm going to stay inside here until you're ready to start expending a little bit more.

41: I hope it stays cool down there for you.

CH: Another day like today and I tell you, I don't know.

41: What all did they hit you with today?

CH: Everything from 57 recoilless to 82 mortars to small arms and, how could I forget the good old B-40 rockets? And I left out the kitchen sink.

41: I've seen a few of those B-40s in my time, too.

CH: I know you have, buddy, I know you have. You're up in world news a little bit. Who's in the limelight here in country? Who's catching the most shit right about now?

41: You boys are catching it, believe me.

CH: Is that right? We're the ones that are catching the most right now in country? I don't know if that makes me feel good or not.

41: Yeah, I just hope this doesn't turn into another Duc Lap like last year.

CH: Old buddy, I'm with you on that.

41: Roger, they had a big arms cache, rice cache down here on the border of II and III Corps on one of the in-route things. It was something like nine tons of rice that they had brought in there.

CH: I know that area. It's been quiet here, and all of a sudden, my God, overnight it just turned into, well, what it is now.

41: Roger that. We were talking about that before we got over here. It kind of reminded us of Duc Lap last year, when we had four Spookys overhead all the time.

CH: I heard Duc Lap caught a little bit the other day.

41: Yeah, they took a little bit. Seems like from our intel reports they were kinda coming in between you there down here and they're kinda spreading out. It's hard to tell what they're gonna do.

CH: Yeah, it sure is. I don't know what it is they want with this firebase, but we'd better get some stuff in here tomorrow or they just might get it.

41: Roger, it suits all the Spooky boys if we could get to stay over here in the daytime, too, but they just won't let us.

CH: I understand that. But I tell you one thing. The most important thing we got going for us at night is you guys upstairs. Let me tell you . . . they know you're up there. Like I said, they're going to stay down and they're not going to mess with us too much. Well, it's a good time to get some sleep now and have some peaceful time. We got a lot of wear and tear here on the boys. They are all holding up pretty good, but I don't know. . . . That battle fatigue is gonna get to a lot of people here pretty soon if this shit doesn't slack off.

41: I know what you mean. You tell all those guys down there we're pulling for you and we're going do what we can from up here.

CH: I don't have to tell them; they already know it, ever since the first night. It really didn't take any building up, because you've been living here with me, like I said, and more.

41: We're gonna try. We were just talking, saying we wish we had everything in the book that we could stay here and drop on those guys, but all we got is beaucoup mini-guns. So, we're gonna use what we got.

CH: As long as you got those, we'll keep their heads down and we'll keep this area safe tonight.

41: We'll be calling you back here in about five minutes and let you start directing us in and we'll see if we can't take care of a few of them for you. (Internal: Man, those guys got it rough down there.) Carbon Outlaw 25, this is Spooky 41 Victor. You gonna have a replacement for us when we start to pull out of target? We'd like to keep something over these boys maybe all night if we can.

Carbon Outlaw 25: We've got you scheduled for a fifteen-minute overlap.

41: Sounds good. These guys have been taking it. As soon as we pull off target and get home we'll be ready to go again.

41: Chickenhawk, Spooky 41.

CH: Spooky 41, this is the Hawk.

41: Roger buddy. Old lady up here is ready to clear us to do a little talking for you.

CH: Okay, real fine. Let's put it to the east of our location . . . southeast and work it on up to the northeast. How's that sound to ya?

41: That sounds good. We're gonna come in right now and drop a flare and we'll start working.

CH: Okay, walk it right into the wood line there if you can.

41: All your friendlies are inside your perimeter there, except the ones to the northwest, is that correct?

CH: That is a definite affirmative.

41: How far to the edge of the wood line do you want us to bring it, over?

CH: I tell you what. You bring it in as close as your little heart desires, right in there, because we get probes during the night and they kinda sneak up there when nobody's watching and I'd like to surprise them.

41: Roger. We've also found out that if we shoot out a couple of hundred meters, it drives them into the perimeter, also, so we'll try to drive them out a little bit.

CH: That's fine, buddy. Use every trick you got.

41: OK, we're coming in hot.

CH: Okay, I'm going out and observe.

41: Hey, Hawk, how we looking baby?

CH: You're looking real fine. I was out there watching you and you're putting it dead in on them. I'd like you to put a few rounds in on the other side of the slopes. I'll explain myself here. Our camp sits here on this hill. Then you go down the hill to the east side, past the wires and you hit the bottom of the hill. Then you hit the dense vegetation and start going up the other side, up the other slopes. During the daytime they're rocketing us from all points around the camp, so at nighttime they might just figure it's safe to pull back to the other side of the hill. So put a few rounds on the other side of the ridge-lines here and maybe we can shake them up a little bit.

41: Okeydoke, we're gonna drop another flare, and we're just gonna start working all around you, babe. Carbon Outlaw 25, this is Spooky 41, we're expending at this time. We'll give you a call when we're half expended.

CH: Hey Spook, this the Hawk. Have you got anybody in to replace you when your time on target is over?

41: You better believe that. We're gonna have a fifteen-minute overlap. And if they'll let us, we'll come back up here tonight as soon we can go and regenerate.

CH: That's what I wanted to hear. You're gonna get some long hours in, aren't you?

41: We don't mind as long as it's helping you boys out.

CH: That's really good. Okay, buddy, that's real fine.

41: Okay, Hawk, we're fixing to move over on the other side of you and work around on those hills a little bit.

CH: Okay, buddy, drive on. Hey, are you hearing those explosions? They sound like they're coming from the west, the southwest.

41: Negative, I haven't heard a thing. What's it sound like, gunfire?

CH: No. It sounds like a distant Arc Light.

41: Roger. You got one down here about ten miles from you.

CH: That's probably what it was then.

41: Roger. If they get to firing on us, we'll shoot at them.

CH: (Laughing) OK.

Carbon Outlaw 25: Spooky 41, how much moonlight do you have down in the area where you are?

41: We have a fair amount of moonlight, but not enough yet to really see the ground yet. We're still having to use flares.

Carbon Outlaw 25: That's a roger, sir. What've you got, a quarter moon, half moon, or a full moon?

41: Roger, stand by just a second. We got about a half moon. And be advised that the ground, you can start to see some mountains, but not real well yet.

Carbon Outlaw 25: Okay, sir, thank you.

41: Hawk, this is 41.

CH: This is the Hawk—go.

41: Roger, old buddy. You know how the trees come up to the north and then kinda cut off these two little bald mountains, just north of your position?

CH: Roger, roger, only too well.

41: We're gonna work that over a little bit if that's all right with you.

CH: Fine, fine, go ahead.

41: And where else would you like for us to move? We're trying to work over all the little peaks and ridgelines around you.

CH: Listen, if you hit the peaks and ridgelines around here that'll be fine.

41: Roger, can you tell me if my bullets are hitting the ground?

CH: Roger, wait one.

41: Hey, Hawk, I'm just kidding you.

CH: Goddammit, buddy, you had me going on that one, I'll say that.

41: I figured I would. Hawk, we're down to about half a load right now. What we're gonna do is stay up here for about forty minutes and just orbit the area. Then we'll come back in and work off the other half of our load and stay with you up to pretty close to two o'clock.

CH: Okay, when you come back in to work off that other half, don't work it all off, in case something happens.

41: You know it; we're gonna save some. And if you want to rest a little bit, we're watching up for any muzzle flashes or anything else, so we'll keep you posted if we see anything. I'll leave you alone for about twenty or thirty minutes and then I'll have a little commo check with you.

CH: 41, this the Hawk, go.

41: I was just talking to 25 and he says that there's a Shadow 64, I believe it is, that's coming in here in about twenty or thirty minutes, so he's going to give us a call when he's about twenty minutes out and we'll come back in and expend all of ours and let him relieve us. We'll go back home and regenerate, probably launch, and come on back up.

(At this point Lt. Mike Smith, call sign "Beak," took over for Captain Albracht.)

Beak: 41, this is Chickenhawk's buddy, over.

41: Roger, Chickenhawk buddy. We're going to be dropping a flare here in about three or four minutes then I'll find targets again, start expending, then we've got Shadow 48 should be on target in about fifteen minutes and we'll point out to him. Also, be advised, we've got another friend up above here, gonna sniff around a little bit and see what he can find for us. And we've already put in a request with our highers trying to get permission for us to regenerate and come back over and stay the rest of the night with you.

Beak: We sure like having you with us. Thanks a lot, over.

41: Break, break, Chickenhawk, Spooky 41, or Chicken-hawk's buddy, Spooky 41, over.

Beak: This is Chickenhawk's buddy.

41: Chickenhawk's buddy, we're ready to shoot.

Beak: Pour it on there, buddy.

41: Roger.

CH: Spooky 41, Spooky 41 this is the Hawk, over. I'll be back here only for a little while, I gotta get some shut eye here. Hey, listen, I'll talk you in. And when you come back—and I hope you do   with this new guy coming in, will you brief him on what you been doing and what you've been shooting, because you're doing an outstanding job there on your own putting it in where you think it's good, and that's exactly where we need it.

41: I've already given him a small rundown, but we're gonna wait for him and show him the area and brief him real good. We've put in a request to turn us around as soon as we get back and we hope our highers will let us come back and spend the night with you. Might not hurt to put a little fire around those fires burning down there. They might be cooking up fish heads and rice with them.

Beak: That's it. We'll starve them so-and-so's out. We decided to change my call sign here, to call me the Beak. I took a piece of shrapnel through the nose. We thought you'd get a kick out of that.

41: You took a piece of shrapnel through the nose?

Beak: That's affirmative. So from now on you can just call me the Beak.

41: Okay, Beak. How bad was it?

Beak: Oh, it just made a nice little neat hole clean through.

41: (Internal: Hey, I got a flash.) Well, maybe the boys can fix you up. Hey, be advised, we just got a flash on the ground.

Beak: Pour it on, pour it on. Get that son of a bitch.

41: Roger, he's to your east on the ridgeline, over there. We're pouring it in on him now.

Beak: Where you're putting on is where we've been receiving a lot of the stuff from today. All over the east side is where we're getting the bulk of it. Go ahead, bring some smoke on his young ass.

41: (Internal: Flare on the [unintelligible] spot here. That was a nice little, looked like a mortar tube flash to me. Internal 2: Yes sir, that's what it looked like to me.) Hey, Beak, did you all take any incoming coming in?

Beak: Hey, 41, this is the Hawk. Negative on that, we didn't take anything incoming, so I think you got a secondary.

41: Might have, cause it sure looked like a mortar splash.

Beak: That's real fine. I hope so, buddy, I hope so. That's one more crew served we won't have to contend with tomorrow.

41: Shadow's coming along with some equipment on board that he might be able to pick out some of this stuff a little better than we can.

Beak: He'll have to show me.

41: He's a second-generation Spooky.

Beak: Okay, I'd say he's got some real fine sophisticated stuff. The country boys are going to have to take a backseat sometimes. But I don't know. I'm from Missouri—Show Me, right?

41: He's going to do you a fine job, so no sweat. (Internal: We got a flare . . .)

Beak: I've no doubt of it, no doubt whatsoever.

41: We're all trying to do the same thing. We're fixing to drop a flare. We got one out right now. We're going to go ahead and expend our ammo. We're getting pretty short, and we're going to try to get Shadow to come up here in just a minute real quick and show you this and then we're going to have to pull out of the area for just a few minutes.

Shadow 48: We're going to hold here north and we've seen the base down there, so we'll be working with you after this other activity is over.

41: Say Beak, we're gonna finish up here.

CH: Go ahead, pour it on, 41.

41: Roger, Beak. We just expended all our rounds and we're gonna move north for a few minutes and watch the action go on. When we leave, Shadow will be coming back in here in a little bit.

Beak: Roger that. Shadow 48 is going to take your place. It was great having you guys here and that's an outstanding job getting that secondary. We get all kinds of hell from that area. I heard you inform Shadow 48 about it.

41: Like I say, he's got some pretty cute little things on board there and he might be able to pick up some things that we don't see. So maybe he can help you out some more. We're gonna go regenerate and try to be back over and relieve him.

Beak: 41, it's been outstanding having you here. The welcome mat's always open, and we'll be looking for you little later.

41: Roger that. Keep your nose down there, buddy

CH: 41, this is the Hawk. I hope I see you little later on. You come back in, and when you get back on . . . you say hi to me, OK?

41: Yeah, we'll do that. And, hey, you tell your buddy to keep his nose down.

CH: His comment was "No shit."

41: (Laughing) I'll bet his comment was that. We're going to move north and get out of the way of some stuff going on, OK?

Welcome Back, Spooky 41

True to his word, Spooky 41 returned. This time, the plane stayed around until daylight, but not much else happened. Dykes recalled coming in after the fighter strikes in daylight and noticed B-40 rockets being fired right into Kate.

41: (Whispering) Chickenhawk, Chickenhawk, do you read?

CH: (Whispering) Roger.

41: (Whispering) This is the Spooky, we're back. How's everything down there?

CH: Real fine. Not to shake you up or anything, but we're going to be firing some direct artillery from the north. It's going to be direct fire, like a bullet, so don't worry, no altitude or nothing.

41: Roger, you got something going on?

CH: A little preventive medicine, you might say. Let me know when you get in a little closer. We just had some resupply in. About six choppers came in, and we opened up for them and gave them ground cover and everything. Now everybody's reloading magazines and cleaning up their weapons.

41: Am I gonna talk to the Hawk tonight or the Beak this time?

CH: While you're up in the area, you'll be talking to both of us.

41: How would you like to work this target? We plan to stay with you today until daylight.

CH: Wish you could stay with us until tomorrow night.

41: We'll probably be back tomorrow night.

CH: Wish you could stay with us the whole time through.

41: I do too. We like to shoot in the daytime.

CH: Yeah, I bet you would there. Have you got a target for me or am I gonna give it to you?

41: We're gonna work for you tonight.

CH: Okay. Let's dump some of your good ordnance around the perimeter one time. In case they got any notion to sneaking up here now, it'll discourage them a little of that. And, let me know if you pick up anything noteworthy as you're going around, okay?

41: How about working it about the same way we did before? We'll expend for a little while and then we'll just hang loose for a while.

CH: Roger, that's just the way I'd like it.

41: Be advised that we will leave here between Zero Six Thirty [6:30 A.M.] and Zero Seven Hundred [7 A.M.]. We're gonna come in here in just a second and start raking around the camp.

CH: Real fine. Just keep it up right there at the interval that you know best, okay?

41: We're gonna make it stretch out till daylight.

CH: Listen, buddy. I'm going to knock it off for tonight. I'm going to go catch a few Zs. It's been a pleasure working with you, and I hope I catch you tomorrow night, okay?

41: Who'll I be working with now, the Beak?

CH: I think you'll be working with Peeper 38.

41: Okay. Is he down there in the same area you are?

CH: He's in the same place I am right now.

41: Been nice working for you. You did a real good job down there and hope you get some good sleep.

CH: So do I. If all my pilots were like you, I'd have no troubles at all. Vote of thanks to all you guys tonight. We'll see you tomorrow night, okay buddy?

As it turned out, Albracht and Dykes would not work together the next night. There would be a Spooky on station, but it would be covering an E&E, rather than just keeping the NVA at bay. That was all Albracht wanted: air support to give his troops a chance to evacuate Kate with minimal losses.

Chapter 14

A Dustoff and
a Surprise

*"The guns and the bombs, the rockets and the warships,
are all symbols of human failure."*

—LYNDON B. JOHNSON

There were two helicopter missions of note on October 31. One involved a medevac flight by two veteran pilots. The other was the resupply mission (see Chapter 12) that was critical for the defenders at Kate. Both were successful, which was a tribute to the helicopter pilots' skills and bravery.

The Vietnam War posed a unique logistical challenge to the military leaders. It was fought in triple-canopy jungle terrain and bad weather. There were constant guerilla attacks. The front line changed from day to day. Often, vehicles were subject to landmines, ambushes, and poor road conditions; some of the areas where heavy fighting took place were so remote there were no roads. All of these factors posed a major problem for the military: how to transport wounded troops safely and quickly to the aid stations and hospitals for proper medical care. To resolve it, the U.S. Army's medical branch decided to revisit an idea that came about in the Korean War—a helicopter ambulance corps. The idea was implemented with so much success in Vietnam that in most cases a wounded soldier would be in a hospital receiving medical care within thirty-five minutes of being wounded.

In April 1962, the 57th Medical Detachment (Helicopter Ambulance) arrived in Vietnam with five UH-1 "Huey" helicopters. They took the call sign Dustoff. Over time the number of medevac detachments grew in Vietnam until the entire country had coverage and Dustoff became the universal call sign for all medevac missions.

A Dustoff crew consisted of four people: two pilots, a medic, and a crew chief. Usually, one pilot would fly the helicopter while the other acted as the aircraft commander. The commander would navigate, monitor all the radio transmissions, talk to the unit requesting the medevac, and take over flying if the pilot were injured. The medic kept the helicopter stocked with the necessary medical supplies and the crew chief maintained the helicopter in top working condition. They would both load the patients onto the helicopter. The medic administered any necessary medical treatment on the way to the hospital, often with the help of the crew chief. The medic and crew chief generally stayed with a particular helicopter, while the pilots were interchangeable between helicopters. These crews saved many lives and were universally respected by all of the soldiers in the war.

A Peculiar Breed

Dustoff pilots were a unique breed. They flew missions that other pilots were loath to undertake. Often, they did so without protection of any kind. Chopper pilot Ken Donovan recalled one mission around Kate during which he flew cover for Dave Bennett, a highly regarded Dustoff pilot. "I always had great respect for the Dustoff crews," Donovan stated. Speaking specifically of one mission he and Bennett flew together, he said, "What the crew of Dustoff 61 did that day was certainly in keeping with the respect that all Dustoff crews had earned." Bennett and his crew certainly earned additional respect—as did Donovan—during the mission to which Donovan alluded.

Sometime in October 1969, Donovan reported, before the action at Kate intensified, his unit was flying single-ship resupply missions in and around Buprang when he got a call for a medevac mission. He asked over his UHF radio if there were any gunships in the area. For some reason, during that time there were none in the vicinity. Where was a gunship when you needed it?

Donovan explained that the first time he tried to land in the zone set up for their arrival, the ARVNs who had not been wounded panicked and swarmed the aircraft to the point where he could not take off. Based on experience and stories he had heard about other pilots crashing when they tried to take off when overloaded, Donovan knew he had to be cautious. He gave his crew members an order to beat the panicking ARVNs off if necessary.

Donovan finally managed to get off the ground and lifted the injured troops back to Buprang. Given the overall situation, he was very concerned about getting out the three wounded Americans who remained.

Back at Buprang, Dave Bennett showed up in Dustoff 61. Donovan explained the situation to him and indicated that there were no gunships available to provide cover for him. But he volunteered to return to the landing zone with Bennett and give him as much cover as he could as the Dustoff pilot made his approach and pickup. Then Donovan would go in and make another pickup.

Bennett and his crew never hesitated. The two pilots started to move the entire ARVN company. As they did, the NVA troops in the area engaged Bennett and Donovan during their approaches, mostly with small-arms fire. They also fired two or three rocket-propelled grenades at Bennett's chopper.

The two pilots coordinated the attempt to get the injured troops back to Buprang. Bennett asked Donovan how he was going back. Donovan indicated that he was returning at low level. Bennett, on the other hand, said he was going back at altitude—which was up to two miles high. At that point they parted company.

Despite the withering enemy gunfire, the two got all three Americans out. Bennett carried the two U.S. advisors who were hit the worst. Donovan ferried one American and two or three ARVNs back with him.

The NVA Was Full of Surprises

They had not been en route very long when Donovan heard Bennett calling on the radio that he was taking 37mm antiaircraft fire near LZ Kate at 10,000 feet. Needless to say, Donovan was somewhat concerned about Bennett and his crew. He needn't have worried. Bennett made it back—with a number of holes all over his aircraft.

Donovan and Bennett spoke later that day after the completion of their mission. Donovan thanked Bennett for his help, although neither one of them thought the mission was a big deal; it was just something that came up to which they reacted. Other people who heard about the mission reacted as well. It was a surprise to some of them that the NVA was using 37mm antiaircraft weapons in the area.

Several soldiers and pilots thought that the report of 37mm weapons in that part of Vietnam was rare. Bennett's revelation was just one more of the surprises friendly forces received around Kate. They were amazed at the variety of weapons the NVA was using. Even though there was some doubt that it did use 37mm weapons, history proves that these weapons were in play.

The official history of the Vietnamese artillery command reports that in 1969 in the Central Highlands front the NVA had two battalions of 37mm AA guns in use. During the year these battalions, along with several other artillery units, were disbanded because of logistics/supply problems. The history reveals that at least some of the 37mm guns were reassigned to several composite artillery battalions subordinate to the 40th Artillery Regiment. Bennett was not imagining things.

The same held true for the NVA's use of 105mm or larger howitzers. Reports from Kate on November 1 stated that the defenders were taking 105 fire. According to a Special Forces after-action report, that was a major concern:

> On 1 November, FSB Kate reported receiving 105mm or larger howitzer fire. This report increases the possibility that elements of the 40th NVA Artillery Regiment are operating in the Bu Prang-Duc Lap area. The 40th NVA Artillery Regiment is the only known unit operating in II CTZ with this type of

artillery weapons. Intelligence reports received during the past four months have indicated that the enemy may be infiltrating 105mm howitzers and possibly 85mm field guns into the Nam Lyr Base Area. Such artillery pieces were used against Camp Ben Het during the May–June siege.

Just One More Weapon to Worry About

Guns like 105mm howitzers were not a problem for helicopter pilots, but they did represent one more danger for the defenders on Kate. The more weapons the NVA deployed to pound ground troops and helicopters alike, the harder it became to sustain operations on Kate. The increasing difficulties did not seem to faze the pilots, however.

One trait that helicopter pilots in Vietnam shared was their willingness to undertake dangerous missions to protect friendly troops—especially if they were Americans. In fact, Donovan commented about the mission that, "I guess the thing I am most proud of is that we were able to save three Americans that day."

The pilots did not have to know what nationality the imperiled troops were or even know them personally. All they needed to hear was that friendly troops needed their help. That was one of the reasons they performed so admirably at Kate where, ironically, Bennett reported taking fire on the mission described above. It was, for him and his fellow pilots, a harbinger of things to come at Kate, whether they were flying in daytime or at night.

Chapter 15

Night Flight

*"Kate was not the scariest part of my combat tour in Vietnam,
but it was surely a chapter that I am proud of. I believe there is
a very small distinction between being a hero and a statistic.
The fact we are alive to tell the story makes us heroes."*

—MIKE WILCOX

Flying at night was never easy. Flying at night under heavy fire was downright difficult, no matter how experienced the pilot was or how well armed a chopper might have been. The perils were myriad, as Ben Gay's experiences near Kate stressed. By the night of October 31, any chopper pilot assigned to fly there cringed.

Gay, a pilot with the 48th Assault Helicopter Company, provided a description of what flying choppers was like in Vietnam. His call sign was—and still is—Joker 73. He was assigned to provide gunship support as the commander of his aircraft and the fire team leader of two UH-1C gunships in support of the mission at the Buprang Special Forces compound and Kate. The firebase and Special Forces compound had been under siege by several NVA divisions, comprising thousands of enemy soldiers.

Armed to Fly

The armament on Gay's aircraft consisted of a rocket pod on each side of the aircraft. Each pod held nineteen 2.75-inch (the diameter of the rocket) rockets, with either a ten-pound or seventeen-pound high-explosive warhead. The rockets were approximately five and a half feet long and would reach the speed of sound in less than two seconds when fired. The rockets were fired in pairs by the pilot in the right-hand seat of the aircraft, who would normally be the aircraft commander. Additionally, each of the two crew members in the back was armed with a 7.62mm M60 machine gun. Each one had two to three thousand rounds of ammunition for his gun, with a rate of fire of approximately 600 rounds per minute.

The second aircraft was armed with a seven-shot rocket pod on each side and a 7.62mm mini-gun on each side. The mini-guns could fire between 4,200 and 6,000 rounds per minute per gun, and the aircraft carried approximately 12,000 rounds of ammunition for the two weapons. The rockets were fired by the pilot in the right seat; the mini-guns were fired by the pilot in the left seat. The two crew members in the back also had the M60 machine guns.

The Pilot and the FAC

Once Gay and his choppers arrived in the area, they contacted the U.S. Army Forward Air Controller (FAC), who was in an O-1 "Bird-dog" fixed-wing aircraft circling above the battlefield. The FAC's mission was to coordinate the combat assaults by the 48th AHC, the effort to get ground troops into Kate, the air strikes by the U.S. Air Force fighter/bombers, and additional close air support by helicopter gunships and resupply helicopters from the 155th AHC.

The skies were crowded around Kate. In addition to the fire teams and lift helicopters from the 48th AHC and the 155th AHC, there were helicopter gunships/fire teams from several other units in the area supporting the Special Forces camp and firebase.

One day, after the pilots' initial contact with the FAC to advise him they were on station in the area of Buprang and Kate, they were assigned the mission of escorting a combat lift by five slicks—UH-1H lift helicopters (troop-carrying helicopters)—into Kate. These aircraft were also from the 48th AHC. Their mission was to insert infantry ground forces into the firebase. Gay's copilot was 1st Lt. Ken Ryder, who was fresh out of flight school had been in-country only one month.

Talk about Multitasking

During the operation they communicated from aircraft to aircraft by their VHF radios, with the FAC by their UHF radios, and with the ground commanders by FM radio. It was not unusual for all three radios to be going at once, each one with an urgent message or request to a pilot or another aircraft, while the crew was engaged in combat.

In addition, the pilot might be receiving information through the aircraft intercom system from crew members in the back and trying to fly the aircraft, operate the weapon systems, and dodge enemy ground fire all at the same time. As Gay exclaimed, "And people think they have to multitask today!"

The combat lift they were going to put in Kate was in response to the extensive ground attacks by the NVA the preceding days against both Buprang and Kate. They met the 48th slicks as they departed the pickup zone (PZ) and escorted them into the landing zone (LZ).

The 48th AHC was able to make the initial insertion of ground forces into the firebase even though the slicks and both aircraft of Gay's fire team came under heavy enemy antiaircraft ground fire from small arms and .51-caliber heavy machine guns. RPGs were also being fired at the slicks by the NVA gunners as the aircraft were on the short final approach for the landing zone at Kate.

The slicks then returned to the PZ, where they loaded for another combat lift into the firebase. They returned to Kate, but the slicks were unsuccessful in the first two attempts to get into the base because of the heavy AA ground fire, which continued despite the intense rocket and machine-gun fire from U.S. gunships and the artillerymen on Kate, who were firing high-explosive and "beehive"/flechette rounds directly into the jungle in the area whence the AA ground fire was originating. (Flechette rounds are pointed steel projectiles with a vaned tail for stable flight. They are capable of piercing armor.)

It was getting dark and the slicks were finally able to get the troops into Kate despite the heavy AA ground fire, which did not let up. Each aircraft sustained damage. Nevertheless, all of them continued to fly.

Flying Blind

After the slicks had departed from Kate, they joined Gay's fire team in a trail formation for the flight back to Ban Me Thuot airfield. By that time, night had set in. It was completely dark, with no ground lights for reference, and clouds had moved into the area. The choppers took up a northeast heading, as there were no navigational aids, air traffic controllers, or other external means of navigating back to Ban Me Thuot in the dark. To compound matters, they were in a very mountainous area of Vietnam, with unreliable maps.

As they flew northeast they started receiving sporadic ground fire from the enemy forces that had surrounded the entire area of the Buprang Special Forces camp and Kate. The pilots were flying at what they thought was 1,000 to 1,500 feet actual ground level, but they could not be sure of their exact elevation in relation to the ground due to the inaccurate maps and the mountainous environment they flew over.

There was an eerie, ethereal quality to the flight. The ground fire appeared as sparkling lights, and occasionally a green tracer would reach up for Gay. The tracers looked initially like small green dots. But, as they rose up from the ground and came closer, they appeared to be the size of basketballs as they went past the aircraft. The unsettling part was knowing there were four other rounds in between each tracer that they could not see.

It was obvious to Gay that the enemy could see his chopper's position lights on the aircraft, but he could not turn them off because of the close proximity of the seven aircraft in the formation and the risk of a midair collision in the clouds and darkness.

The choppers soon cleared the area of the enemy forces, but a new problem developed. The flight lead for the slicks informed Gay that his flight was very low on fuel. About ten minutes later the slick flight lead contacted Gay again and informed him that his twenty-minute fuel warning light had illuminated, which indicated the aircraft would run out of fuel in approximately twenty minutes. The other four slick aircraft pilots indicated they were in the same fuel situation.

Lead Me toward the Light

Gay and his wingman still had sufficient fuel for approximately forty-five minutes to an hour. As they flew along they were in and out of the clouds. Gay was not sure of his exact height above the mountains, or if he was going to collide with another chopper at any moment. To complicate matters, he was not sure of his exact location. He wondered whether he was headed towards Ban Me Thuot or if he had wandered across the border into Cambodia.

Admittedly, Gay was extremely nervous, to say the least. He looked over to his copilot, but Lieutenant Ryder appeared like he did not have a worry in the world. He sat in the left seat smoking a cigar. As far as Gay could see, Ryder had no idea what a serious situation they were in. Gay could not help but think these were their last moments on earth.

Approximately fifteen minutes later, the slick flight lead contacted Gay and said he was down to five minutes of fuel and would have to land in the next several minutes. If he did not land, and the aircraft ran out of fuel in the dark over the mountains, it would be sure death for everyone aboard.

Gay looked down just as the slick pilot delivered his dire news. Through the haze of the clouds he saw what appeared to be a single light below. He radioed the slick lead, whose flight of five aircraft was still in a trail formation behind his fire team, and informed him of this development.

Gay admitted he did not know exactly where the light was, what it was, or whose it was. But, he said, landing there would be the only chance for him and the other nineteen crewmen on the five aircraft to survive. The slick pilot had to make a decision fast. He would be coming up on the light in a few seconds.

Slick lead stated he saw the light and his flight would attempt to land at this location. Gay did not know if he would ever hear from or see any of the crewmen on those aircraft again.

A "Flare" for the Dramatic

Gay and his partner continued to fly for another fifteen to twenty minutes before he was able to make radio contact with the 155th AHC flight operations at Ban Me Thuot. He took up a heading he thought would be the right direction to Ban Me Thuot. By that time, Gay had come out of the clouds and haze. He asked the 155th operations to have someone fire flares into the air. If he was heading in the right direction he might see them. It worked; he saw the flares.

Twenty to twenty-five minutes later, Gay and his partner were landing at the home of the 155th AHC at Ban Me Thuot. They learned later that night that the light he had seen was at the Duclap U.S. Special Forces camp. The troops there had radioed the 155th AHC operations that all five aircraft had landed at their compound without further incident.

Gay found a place to lay over for the night. The next day he began all over again, as if nothing unusual had occurred. Such were the conditions other chopper pilots faced on Halloween night as they flew a desperate resupply mission to Kate.

Assigned Volunteers

It was evident to everyone but Albracht by the night of October 31 that they could not hold out at Kate much longer. He had absolutely no intention of abandoning the base until the Yards advised him that Mike Force could not reinforce them. "This was my first command, and I was not going to give it easily to the NVA," he stressed. In fact, he did not give any thought to evacuating Kate until the afternoon of

November 1. When he finally requested permission to abandon Kate, he told the authorities, "We are no longer defending an impact area; we ceased to be a firebase a couple days ago."

But, as he learned quickly, he was on his own. There were no additional reinforcements available for Kate or aircraft to insert them. If Albracht was going to lead the troops to safety, he would have to do so with the troops and supplies he had at hand. His predicament led to some speculation following the escape from Kate that the South Vietnamese commanders in charge of the firebases were reluctant to commit any more of their available troops to defending them.

There was a good bit of fighting in the region, and the troops might be needed elsewhere. So, for all intents and purposes, the troops on the firebases were left to their own devices. They would have to rescue themselves.

Meanwhile, plans were set in motion elsewhere in case Albracht needed supplies to help him evacuate the base. The 155th AHC was chosen to provide them. Despite the dangers involved in a resupply mission at night, the members of the company were willing—and eager—to carry it out.

As reported in chapter 12, on the evening of October 31 Maj. Dean M. Owen, commanding officer of the 155th AHC, received a call to the District Headquarters in Ban Me Thuot. He was briefed on the dire tactical situation at Kate. Owen learned that the base was surrounded by enemy forces and plans were being made to evacuate it. The fact that he was being asked to conduct an emergency night resupply mission to provide small-arms ammunition to the occupants told him this was no ordinary mission.

As he and all his pilots were aware, night operations were very unusual and hazardous. Nevertheless, Owen knew he had no choice: he had to send his pilots on this mission. The lives of 150 soldiers were at stake. And, so he thought, were the lives of his pilots and crews.

But that is why men and women serve in the military: to risk their lives to complete a mission and save others when they can. He ordered his pilots and crew members to prepare for the unusual and risky operation.

Slicks and Gunships

Nine choppers were assigned to the mission: five UH-1H helicopters and four UH-1C gunships. Owen volunteered himself as flight lead for the resupply aircraft, with WO James Abbott as the pilot. Warrant Officer John "Les" Davison was the flight lead for the armed aircraft. The thirty-six men who flew the mission were an unusual mix of warrant officers, commissioned officers, and enlisted personnel. When it came to saving their fellow soldiers' lives, ranks did not matter to these men.

Owen knew that the pilots were not going to be able to fly into Kate undetected, land, drop off their supplies, and fly away unmolested. The operation had to be coordinated carefully with the troops aboard Kate. Therefore, because of the difficulty in making an unassisted night landing, the pilots' plan was to approach to a hover, then have two Special Forces soldiers in the rear quickly unload the cases of ammunition. The plan worked to perfection—to everyone's surprise.

You Have Been Selected . . .

Ken Donovan, one of the resupply slick pilots, has vivid memories of the night the emergency resupply mission into Kate took place. Due to the large number of supporting aircraft at Ban Me Thuot City Airfield he was moving aircraft over to Ban Me Thuot East Field as a protective measure because of an increasing number of NVA mortar attacks.

As Donovan was flying an aircraft over to Ban Me Thuot East Field, he received a call to report to operations as soon as possible. When he walked into operations, he noticed several other very senior aircraft commanders already there. Someone indicated they were going to conduct an emergency resupply into Kate. The information really got his attention.

Donovan and his fellow pilots knew that the entire area around Kate and Buprang was like the Wild West and the Shootout at the OK Corral. The area had a large number of NVA 12.7mm antiaircraft positions. One Dustoff pilot, Dave Bennett (Dustoff 62), had taken

37mm fire near Kate at 10,000 feet earlier. That in itself caught some soldiers by surprise.

The overall situation had gotten so bad that aircraft had not been able to get into Kate for about the last forty-eight hours. That was bad for the flight crews, but it was worse for the troops on the base. The large number of ground attacks resulted in a severe shortage of small-arms ammo, hence the need to resupply Kate.

There was some discussion at the meeting of using sling loads to get the ammo into Kate. Much to everyone's relief, Owen killed that bad idea rather quickly.

Owen then indicated the 155th had been tasked with an emergency resupply of Kate. The assembled aircraft commanders would be flying, and they had the pick of the rest of the unit for their pilots. Donovan would fly with Jim Hitch, who had been shot down on his first mission in Vietnam the previous August. Hitch had handled his baptism of fire okay, so Donovan figured he was a good choice. Owen indicated there would be another briefing for all pilots later.

Specialist 5 Mike Wilcox, 2nd Flight Platoon, 155th AHC, received an invitation to the party, too. He was not quite prepared for the mission, but he was willing to take part, as were his buddies. He recalled that on the night of the resupply into Kate, the 1st and 2nd Platoon crew chiefs and door gunners were well into a "drink-a-thon" in their barracks area. This was not an unusual activity once the aircraft maintenance was complete and the guards had been posted on the perimeter. They gathered in the 2nd Platoon hooch where they had constructed a bar a few months earlier. Although the troops had all been very active flying missions in the Buprang area and the surrounding firebases, they assumed the war was over for the day, and the Schlitz and Falstaff were tasting really good.

At the time, they had been without a hard-stripe platoon sergeant for over a month. He had gone home on leave and not returned. The platoon had sorted itself out and Wilcox started doing some of the technical inspections and overseeing enlisted crew and aircraft assignments in addition to his regular crew chief duties on aircraft 540 as part of Ken Donovan's crew.

Wilcox was sure they didn't need a hard-striper. "The platoon was made up of a really great bunch of guys, and in some ways ran better without a hard-stripe NCO in charge," he remembered. Then again, the lack of one did not bother him terribly. Wilcox was getting really short on his combat tour; he was scheduled to return home in less than a month, at Thanksgiving. He did not have to fly given his new duties, but he was getting a bit itchy. Wilcox had been passing the days by scheduling himself for missions that would avoid the boring mail runs for MACV (Military Assistance Command, Vietnam).

Wilcox craved a little excitement. He noted that missions into the Buprang area were guaranteed to pass the day quickly, as there were a very large number of "bad guys" in the region. In fact, he said, the gunfights in the Kate area were at a level where the crews could actually see large numbers of dead NVA soldiers lying in the open. "Being young and bulletproof, it was an exciting way for me to pass the day," he said. "Looking back on it forty-four years later, with grown kids and grandkids, flying the mail runs would have been the better choice." But, as wise men say, the past is prologue. Wilcox and his buddies sensed that some friendlies were in trouble, and they needed help. Into the tiger's lair they went.

Sometime well after dark, Wilcox received his summons to operations, which was somewhat unexpected. "As soon as I entered operations," he said, "I could sense a buzz of urgency and that something unusual was about to happen. From my experience of flying in the Buprang and LZ Kate area over the last several days, I knew the overall situation was becoming increasingly difficult."

The briefing officers advised the assembled crews of the mission and presented them with two initial plans: Plan A and Plan B. Plan A was to load ammo and supplies in cargo nets and lift them utilizing the Hueys' cargo hooks, and then drop them on Kate. The mention of cargo hooks jolted Wilcox for the moment. "A word about having a cargo hook on your aircraft," he explained. "To avoid having to fly resupply missions all the time and to save weight, most of the crew chiefs had removed the cargo hooks from the aircraft. I was asked to see how many aircraft with cargo hooks we could get ready." Dutifully, Wilcox returned to the platoon area and grabbed as many somewhat sober crewmen as he could. He located several cargo hooks in the maintenance storage area, and in a very short time the crews had completed installing them on the required number of aircraft.

About the time they were done, they were informed of Plan B, which was to load the ammo and supplies in the doorways of the aircraft, through which two Special Forces guys would kick the ammo out over Kate on a spot marked by a strobe light buried in the ground. It did not really matter to Wilcox and his buddies how the ammo reached the ground, as long as it got there—and they knew that it could very well be their fates to hit the ground with it. "When I was told to ask for volunteers only to fly the mission, I knew this was going to be a very difficult mission," Wilcox admitted. "I was told that it was expected to be very ugly in terms of possible aircraft loses." And he emphasized, "Not one of the platoon guys from the 155th knew any of the guys on the ground at LZ Kate. But, as soon as I requested volunteers I was amazed to see that every crewman was ready and willing to go—and suddenly very sober." In fact, he concluded, "We could have manned more than one mission if necessary."

Wilcox was not going to miss the show. He assigned himself to fly with Ken Donovan, his regular aircraft commander, who had been assigned to fly in Chalk 4, the last slick in the formation going into Kate. Wilcox, like everyone else on the mission, was apprehensive about the outcome. "I remember the approach into Kate," he offered. "It was not as fast as I would have liked. I knew we were sitting ducks if the NVA decided to open up. I still can't understand why they never fired during our approach into Kate. We completed our part of the resupply mission and returned to base." He returned the following night on another resupply mission. That was the night of the E&E. Wilcox would never forget either mission. "What really counts for me and what I remember most is our willingness to risk our lives for another American soldier in trouble. Without our faith in each other, and our willingness to risk ourselves for each other, missions like LZ

Kate could have never occurred—at least not without a chance of success." That was the prevailing attitude around Kate—and explains why so many of the troops involved lived to tell about it.

An All Too Brief Briefing

At that second briefing, the overall game plan was announced: the ammo-carrying slicks would report to Ban Me Thuot East Field to pick up ammo and two Special Forces personnel per slick to kick the ammo out. There were four ammo-carrying slicks. (Donovan flew as Chalk 4). Four Falcon gunships escorted them, two on either side of the formation. The fifth slick went along as an overall command-and-control and recovery aircraft.

During the briefing, Owen established himself with Donovan as one of the best commanders of his twenty-eight-year career when he informed the pilots and crews that he would be flying lead with Jim Abbott. That, in their eyes, was a class move and an example of leadership at its best.

After the crews reported to Ban Me Thuot East, the ammo was loaded in the doors and they departed for Kate. For Donovan, the takeoff from Ban Me Thuot East was probably the scariest part of the mission. At about 500 feet they ran into a broken cloud layer and went IFR (Instrument Flight Rules) in formation.

He remembered seeing Chalk 3 flash in and out of the clouds. Abbott, who was in lead, called out "climbing at 60 knots and 500 feet." A short time later they broke out on top of the cloud cover in bright moonlight. By the time they got to Kate, the weather was clear, and it did not play a factor in the rest of the mission.

While en route to Kate, Donovan instructed his crew chief and gunner to give their helmets to the two Special Forces guys so he could brief them on what to do when they got to Kate, and what to do if they got hit and went down. His game plan was easy: if they got hit going in, and there was any doubt about his ability to fly the chopper out of the immediate area, he was going to plant it in the middle of Kate and wait for pickup by the backup slick. He thought at the time if they went down short of Kate, things would have been rather interesting.

As they approached Kate, the flight lead established communication with the guys on the ground. The plan was to shoot an approach to a strobe light that had been placed in a shallow hole in the ground so that it could only be seen from above by an aircraft on approach. Everyone was on edge as they approached. They did not have to be.

Owen was happy to learn that leadership (Albracht and Pierelli) on the ground was organized and professional. "We were given the most recent information available concerning the position of enemy troops and gun emplacements," he observed.

As the resupply choppers approached, an Air Force Spectre gunship (another variation of a C-130, closely related to a Spooky) reported to them that he was moving out of the immediate area. Donovan was happy to hear that. The fact that a Spectre had been working the area was an important element of the mission's success that night. The plane had made the "bad guys" very gun-shy.

During the briefing, there was some discussion as to whether or not the choppers would go in hot (firing) or cold (not firing). The decision was to stay cold until they took fire. During their first approach, the pilots could not see the strobe light for some reason and had to make a go-around. Nothing like announcing to the world "Here we come."

The choppers made a left-hand orbit and came around to line up for their second approach. This time they saw the strobe light and started to descend. Donovan fully expected that at any time the whole area was going to light up. Being Chalk 4, the last guy in, he was not really fired up about this prospect. At the time of this mission, he was on an extension in Vietnam, and had only about thirty days left in-country. J. C. Cole, who was also on the mission, and Donovan were scheduled to leave on R&R the next day. Getting shot down—or worse—the night before would not be good for their psyches.

The gunships provided suppressive covering fires for the helicopters as they swooped in. Donovan watched as each of the first three aircraft made its approach in and out of Kate. He was amazed that the choppers still had not received any fire. As it was, none of them really landed at Kate.

Donovan made his approach down to about twenty feet above the ground. When he saw the strobe light between his feet through the chin bubble, he gave the order to kick the ammo. His next radio call was "Chalk 4 climbing out!"

He told Jim Hitch, "Let me know when I hit forty-eight pounds" and pulled the collective (used for pitch control) up under his armpit. He was still amazed that at no time during the approach or climb out did any aircraft take any fire. And, he was the last one to climb out. That gave him the distinction of being the last aircraft to approach Kate. The next night Albracht E&E'd his entire force out of Kate.

The rest of the mission was rather anti-climatic. As Donovan concluded simply, "We completed the mission without losing an aircraft or sustaining injury to any of the crew members."

The slicks and gunships flew back to Ban Me Thuot still in awe that the "bad guys" had been asleep. As Donovan commented, "I do remember more chatter than usual on the VHF frequency the slicks used to talk to each other."

Cole and Donovan landed, got three or four hours of sleep, got up, and left for R&R. Donovan continued to fly missions for another month or so and ended his combat tour and came home on December 5, 1969. Shortly after he left, the battle of Buprang ended as the NVA forces moved back across the border.

There was a great deal of relief among the crew members of the nine helicopters that completed the mission to resupply Kate. Given the number of NVA around Kate, and the amount of fire choppers in the area took on a daily basis, their mission was one of the most serious—and most essential. They may have been relieved at their own good luck, but they were in a somewhat somber mood.

Most of the men on that mission believed when they took off that they would come back with fewer aircraft than they left with. Nevertheless, all of the air crews climbed into their aircraft willingly, and there was never any question among them of the fact that some of them would not come back. Their successful mission completion was due to luck, skill, and leadership.

To this day, Donovan lauds the great leadership they had at all levels, at the aircraft commander, platoon leader, and company-level command. The same could be said of the troops who were left at Kate. Thanks to the helicopter crew from Ban Me Thuot, the men at Kate had badly needed supplies. It was up to Albracht and Pierelli to get them out of there. They would, but it was not easy.

Day 6

November 1, 1969

Chapter 16

D-Day

"1 November 1969. FB Kate was again attacked and the order was given to evacuate. B Troop supported contact near Kate and Camp Buprang. Gunships and LGHs were credited with 9 KBA late in the afternoon. The elements at FB Kate effected a linkup with forces from Camp Buprang and returned to Camp Buprang."

—7/17 AFTER-ACTION REPORT FOR NOVEMBER 1, 1969

It was apparent to Albracht on the morning of November 1 that the defenders of Kate could not hold out much longer and that they were in increasingly imminent danger of being captured or slaughtered. The month may have changed, but their situation had not. It had gotten worse, if that was possible.

Despite the previous day's resupply, their predicament was tenuous at best. Albracht would have scoffed at a *New York Times* report in its October 31 edition that described the situation at Annie and Kate: "Some allied soldiers have been killed and light damage has been inflicted in the attacks, [a] spokesman said."

The damage was anything but light, and Kate's situation was dire. The NVA made it more precarious on November 1, starting—as usual—early in the morning.

Shrapnel and Shock

Albracht resigned himself to the fact that the defenders would have to fend for themselves that day. The NVA had the base zeroed in. Subsequently, Kate started to take an ever-increasing number of incoming rounds. There was no helicopter support, which made the troops more aware of their vulnerability—and their mortality.

A description in a November 1 *New York Times* dispatch compared the action around Kate to the earlier siege of Benhet: "The clashes up to today in that area—around a Cambodian border panhandle that juts into Quangduc—have resembled the early stages of the build-up around Benhet, where a prolonged artillery battle occurred last summer." The defenders at Kate might have quibbled with the word "clashes." To them, it was the fight of their life, especially as pieces of shrapnel fell all around Kate, and deafening sounds filled the air.

NVA artillery started raining down airbursts from Cambodia, forcing the troops to stay inside their bunkers. At least one soldier reached his breaking point. Specialist Hopkins suddenly got the feeling that they could not be pulled out. The constant incoming and the realization that no ground support would be coming to save the day was too much. "I knew I needed to do something else or I was probably going to perish, which I did not look forward to," he said. "I remember Doc telling me to get hold of myself. I just could not stay inside the bunker, not knowing what was going on around me; Doc had me evacuated."

Hopkins felt both guilty and relieved upon leaving Kate. As he was exiting, he performed one more favor for the defenders who remained behind. As the chopper departed Kate, it was flying right over the site where the a NVA had a .51-caliber machine gun set up. Hopkins informed the pilot of its location. The pilot diverted his flight path, and Hopkins reached safety, wondering if he would be the last man off Kate.

Time to Go

Intelligence indicated that the NVA were preparing for a final, all-out assault on Kate. The NVA's last mission order was to attack on the evening of November 1—and no retreat was authorized. Albracht did not have any way of knowing that at the time, but it would not have made a difference if he had. It finally dawned on him that he had to get the troops off Kate to safety. Confirmation of an impending NVA assault reinforced his decision.

On November 1, a U.S. Air Force reconnaissance aircraft intercepted an NVA message that said a very large force was assembling to overrun the base. That was the final nail in Kate's coffin—hopefully not literally—as far as Albracht was concerned.

Captain Albracht received the order to withdraw at approximately 1830 hours on November 1. The order was a foregone conclusion, at least on his part. He had made up his mind that he was going. It was time to implement an escape-and-evasion plan. First, he had to draw one up.

Albracht assembled the troops after dark in the vicinity of the base's north slope, the only slope that could be easily traversed, to describe the preparation steps for their escape. The other three slopes were very steep, and the firebase force had taken the least amount of enemy fire from the north slope.

As Albracht surveyed the terrain and the assembled troops, he could not help but feel that they were all just dead men walking. To his dismay, the true dead men there would have to stay behind. They could not take out their comrades lying silently in the body bags on Kate. The option simply did not exist. Albracht said a silent prayer for the dead and concentrated on the living.

Dead Men Walking

Outwardly, Albracht portrayed a cool demeanor as a way to instill confidence in his troops. Inwardly, he was not calm. Albracht understood the perils of the operation and the pressure on him and Pierelli to lead the force to safety. They would break out through their own concertina wire and through enemy lines, a difficult challenge for seasoned troops, let alone the mixed force he had at his disposal.

It would have been one thing if he were leading Special Forces troops or trained infantrymen. Instead, the group he would be leading included, as Johnson noted, "a couple of dozen neophyte artillerymen." As a result, Albracht took extra care to make sure everybody understood what was at risk and what they had to do. Their survival depended on Albracht—and many of the men weren't quite sure they would survive at all.

"There seemed to be little likelihood that many of us would be able to escape from Kate without being killed or captured by the NVA," Johnson said. "We placed our lives in Captain Albracht's hands and hoped for the best. We were all prepared to die before midnight on November 1st."

Like Koon, Johnson feared the worst:

> We expected that we must fight our way through the NVA lines since we were 100 percent surrounded—and we expected to incur substantial casualties. Our only chance of success was to focus all of our small-arms firepower on the narrow grassy saddle that lay between LZ Kate and Ambush Hill. With luck and the element of surprise, maybe the bulk of our personnel could overwhelm the NVA troops near this saddle. Once through the NVA lines, the plan was to continue our charge across Ambush Hill seeking the safety of the wood line on the other side of the hill. Captain Albracht stressed that the speed of the charge was critical because the NVA will rapidly close in on our point of attack in the saddle area from both sides.

Even Albracht had his doubts about whether he would survive the night. "Convinced that I would not see another sunrise on this Earth, I made my peace with the Almighty," he revealed. "Once I did that, though, a sense of calmness and well-being came over me. It was time, and I was ready." So were the troops.

Albracht circulated among the men, explaining carefully how they would linkup with Detachment B-20 of Mike Force, which would be waiting for them in a concealed position about three miles away, which was not the original plan. At least Special Forces sent in the best they had—Detachment B-20 of the II Corps Mobile Strike Force (Mike Force), headquartered in Pleiku.

Mike Force planned to deploy a reinforced battalion consisting of three rifle companies from the 1st Battalion and two rifle companies from the 5th Battalion, approximately nine hundred troops. They intended to land on or as close as possible to Kate as a direct reinforcement. That did not happen because of the overwhelming numbers of NVA encircling the base. Mike Force fell back on Plan B.

The primary force received orders to air-assault two companies into the immediate area and secure a position within a few hundred meters of Kate's perimeter to cover the E&E group's withdrawal. Three additional Mike Force companies were to be inserted to block the NVA and provide direct security once the withdrawal had begun. Again, that proved to be impossible.

Ultimately, only two rifle companies (252 and 253) from the 5th Battalion managed to get boots on the ground, but not directly on Kate. Instead, they landed a couple kilometers north-northeast of Kate. The two companies swooped in via helicopter airmobile assault and took up their positions before the NVA could react. It was up to Albracht to find them.

While the Mike Force unit established its position, Albracht repeated over and over that everything was under control and they would be fine. The captain did everything he could to keep up morale. There was no one to offer him any morale boosters, though. The troops looked to him for leadership, and he was responsible for his own morale. But Albracht was too worried about everyone else at that point to think about that.

Chapter 17

Did I Miss Anything?

*"My guess is the Mike Force company was approx 4 k's away,
but we had to move so very slowly in the triple-canopy jungle
due to the NVA that were scouring the area looking for us.
On more than one occasion we had to stop,
hunker down, and let them pass in the darkness."*

—CAPT. WILLIAM ALBRACHT

Darkness enveloped the firebase and heavy clouds blocked whatever moonlight would be available as an eerie quiet came over the area. For the first time in five days, Albracht was not actively involved in defending Kate, and he started reflecting on the situation. He ran through the E&E plan in his mind. The captain was on edge, but he couldn't let anyone else see that.

Albracht listened to the radio for Spooky, to no avail. He wanted to start the E&E immediately, and the waiting was wearing on his mind. He was in a situation he could not control, and he did not like the feeling. And he was missing a critical component of his E&E team: a radio operator.

Radio Operator Needed: Anyone Can Apply

Leading inexperienced troops through unfamiliar terrain at night while being pursued by enemy troops was bad enough. Doing so without radio contact with air cover and rescue forces was impossible. Albracht and Pierelli would have their hands full leading the troops, which did not give them much leeway regarding radio communications. They desperately needed someone to take over as radio operator.

The assignment was especially critical because the radio operator would be in the lead with Albracht. He had to be the captain's shadow—and be able to complement him perfectly. One artilleryman could fit those criteria: a soft-spoken sergeant from Texas named Gerald V. "Tex" Rogers. He volunteered immediately.

Rogers—who would earn a Bronze Star Medal with "V" device for his role in the E&E, the armed forces' fourth-highest award for bravery, heroism, or meritorious service—was well respected by his comrades. He was Koon's section leader, and a man to whom Koon paid serious attention. "We were on the same gun," Koon recalled. "He was a man among men. He was a big, muscular guy who wouldn't take crap from anyone." Koon learned that lesson early. "Everyone knew him as 'Tex.' You didn't want to call him by his first name. I did once and he told me not to do it again or he would kick my ass. Needless to say, I never called him Gerald again."

Tex Rogers was exactly the kind of soldier Albracht needed as a radio operator. He was not afraid of new situations, maintained his composure under duress, and exercised well-developed leadership skills that instilled confidence in his troops. Albracht described Rogers as a natural infantryman: "His leadership and bravery inspired his men, and certainly impressed me. When it became evident that we could no longer sustain the fight, we were given orders to escape and evade as best we could and link up with another unit, at night, and in the jungle. I needed a good man to carry my radio. I did not have to look far."

The Planes, the Planes

That was one problem solved. Another one was making sure the troops were satisfied with the plan. But that did not bother Albracht much. The fact that their lives were on the line provided the all-important incentive the troops needed to follow Albracht's plan. Before they launched it, they experienced a moment of hope that they would not have to walk out after all.

At dusk, the troops on Kate saw a group of helicopters in the distance. They figured that the choppers were coming to get them out. But they were disappointed when they learned that was not the case. The choppers were carrying a Mike Strike Force that was going to drop about approximately two miles from Kate and work its way toward the base which, as events turned out, it did not do.

As the MSF approached Kate, it encountered heavy fire from the NVA. The relief force had to set up a fighting position away from the base. The troops on Kate still had to escape from the base and link up with the MSF. They had work to do first.

Albracht instructed the troops to destroy all personal items except the water, weapons, and small-arms ammunition they could carry. They anticipated fighting their way out, and every bullet was necessary.

The force had to be able to move fast and quietly. The troops waited for dark to prepare for the E&E. Once the light disappeared, they stacked all the ammunition in three separate locations on the firebase: one pile at the north end, one in the center, and one at the south end. Then, they took care of a heartbreaking—but necessary—task: destroying the equipment they could not take with them to deprive the enemy of its use.

Spiking the Tubes

The artillerymen may not have been trained infantrymen, but they knew what to do in an E&E. Johnson implemented the FDC plan to destroy the radios, code books, documents, and all other materials that might have any use to the NVA. Not that the radios mattered, as things turned out: the NVA was monitoring Kate's transmissions on their own radios.

Cannoneers "spiked the tubes" by dropping thermite grenades into them to destroy permanently what was left of the three howitzers. They knew that airstrikes the next morning would destroy the powder and artillery shells. Still, nothing could be left to chance.

He's Everywhere, He's Everywhere

While the troops carried out their preparations, Albracht tended to myriad details. He contacted the relief column to plan how and where to make the linkup following the escape from Kate. He also made arrangements with the air force to provide covering fire throughout the E&E. Finally, he coordinated with the CIDG commanders to prepare an escape plan acceptable to them.

Albracht was well aware that the artillerymen had limited, if any, experience in infantry operations. Therefore, he chose the only escape route that he believed was feasible for the rapid movement at night of 150 men unfamiliar with the terrain and infantry tactics.

He explained the plan in excruciating detail to the leaders and requested that each of them make certain that the personnel in their units understood fully the critical importance of each step in it—and that the NVA would be dogging their steps every inch of the way. Once he was satisfied everyone knew his role in the plan, there was only one thing left to do: implement it.

If I Die before I Wake

Orders went out to meet at the command bunker and prepare to move out. As Koon described the meeting, it was an emotional moment. "Guys were shaking hands with each other, saying that if they don't make it and the other guy does, tell his parents what happened here," he recalled. Reality interrupted their emotional farewells as small-arms fire erupted at the north end of the base.

Albracht said he would check it out. "If I'm not back in five minutes, leave without me," he said. The troops decided quickly that was not going to happen.

"A lot of us decided right then and there that if Captain Albracht didn't return in five minutes, then we weren't going anywhere either," Koon said. "We decided that this was a man we would follow through the gates of hell, and if he didn't return, then we would stay and fight to the end. I'm sure many people wouldn't understand," Koon explained. "But you get this bond in war, a certain camaraderie that those who haven't experienced combat can't comprehend." The issue became moot when Albracht returned from his excursion across the firebase, which was anything but uneventful, and the troops prepared to begin their frenzied descent down the hill.

Before the troops left the firebase, Spads (World War II–era A-1 Skyraiders, single-seat American attack planes) came in and strafed areas along the route between Kate and Ambush Hill. They were not what Albracht had ordered, but any air support at that point was helpful. According to the evacuation plan, Spooky was supposed to be on station to cover the E&E by clearing a path with mini-guns. The troops waited.

The pilot of the first plane called to advise that he had to turn around because of mechanical problems, but said that a replacement was already airborne. The force waited. Then came more disappointment: the second plane's pilot reported an abort for the same reason.

They were waiting for the third plane when Albracht moved down to the south end of Kate and heard troop movement in the wire. The E&E was not off to a good start.

Route, Step

One of the first maneuvers soldiers learn in recruit training is "route step," a normal marching pace in which it is not necessary to walk in step. It is used mainly in the field when troops move from place to place as a unit. At this point, Albracht was more interested in telling everybody about the route he had planned. It was assumed that everybody knew they would not have to march in step. All they had to do was stay together. That proved impossible once they stepped off.

Albracht informed everyone of two key elements of the E&E plan: the withdrawal route and linkup position. He was experienced enough to know that once the move began the troops would lose contact with one another, so it was vital for everyone to know where the linkup position was and the best route to get there.

By 10 P.M., everyone was assembled at the north end of the firebase. Ever the stickler for detail, Albracht made one final check of the base to make sure everyone was ready and nothing of value in operating condition had been left behind for the North Vietnamese. That was the point where Koon and his comrades vowed to stay and fight if the captain did not return.

Albracht was at the south end of the site when he heard NVA personnel just outside the perimeter wire. He recognized that it was time to go—and not a minute too soon. As he started moving toward the north end of the base, night turned into day.

Let There Be Light—But Not Right Now

NVA soldiers fired appropriated U.S. illumination flares that lit the entire base. Albracht theorized that the enemy had probably gotten them from a sling-load of resupply ammo jettisoned from a helo during heavy ground fire earlier in the day, but he couldn't be sure.

"Is one of you trying to get us killed?" Albracht asked himself, thinking that one of his own troops had sent up the round. He checked their 60mm mortar as he passed it, but it had not been fired. He knew immediately that the NVA suspected something was happening, and they wanted to get a look. They were right—and they wasted no time in acting to stop it.

NVA mortar gunners began blanketing the base with rounds. They started dropping mortar shells at the south end, where Albracht had been just moments earlier, and walked their rounds toward the north end, where he was heading, and where his strikers were massed for evacuation.

Albracht made another in his string of command decisions. There was no time to lose at that point, so he announced to the troops that they were leaving without air support—well, almost none. There was finally one Spad on station that had been providing suppressive fire.

The captain asked him to strafe the gap just prior to the troops' departure. The pilot advised that he had only enough fuel for one more strafing run. That was a dilemma for Albracht. If he used the Spad as a preemptive strike on the gap, the plane would have to break off, leaving the escaping troops with no one to intimidate the NVA from the air.

Since Albracht did not know what lay ahead, he decided to hold onto this one remaining asset and wait until they had actual contact from the enemy. In any case, he figured, the mere sound of the Spad above kept the NVA's attention. That alone was worth a few points in his estimation.

Hitting the Slope

Everyone had agreed on a specific route off the firebase and into the no-man's-land of the jungle: the troops, led by a CIDG point team, would go down the north slope, travel through a small gap in the wood line, go up the slope of the next hill, skirt to the left of the hill-top, then head in a west-northwest direction to link up with elements of the 5th Battalion, 2d MSFC. Because it was so dark, each man was instructed to hold on to the web gear of the man in front of him so no one would stray from the column. That was the plan. The adage about the "best-laid plans of men and E&Eers" intervened.

Chapter 18

E&E

"We Gotta Get out of This Place"

—SONG TITLE BY THE ANIMALS

Many songs were popular among the troops in Vietnam: "Run through the Jungle," "Fortunate Son," and "Who Will Stop The Rain" by Credence Clearwater Revival, anything by The Doors, and others. They all remind Albracht of Vietnam today. One song in particular set the theme for the E&E operation at Kate: "We Gotta Get out of This Place" by The Animals.

He Really Didn't Want to Go

Captain Albracht might not have been aware of it at the time, but he really did not want to leave Kate. At least that is what an unidentified colonel told a *New York Times* reporter who, in the November 3 edition, noted that the order to abandon the other camps, besides Buprang, "wasn't what we would have preferred but we couldn't do much about it." As the colonel explained, "The camps actually belonged to the

South Vietnamese. Our people were in them only in supporting or advisory roles and so they had no say."

Fortunately, the captain did not have the time to read newspapers. Nor would he have agreed with the colonel. He was much closer to the situation. And he was ready to leave.

Let the Rush Begin

At about 10 P.M., Albracht shouted the command the troops had long awaited: "Get out!" They started a mad dash through the perimeter wire at the north end of the field and down the slope. Albracht was right where he always was: near the front, even though he was still weary from his three-day-old wounds. Pierelli, the other experienced troop leader and combat soldier, was toward the rear of the column.

The E&Eers did not need to hear Albracht's order a second time. Just as they began their rush, one CIDG striker fell almost immediately, killed by a mortar shell. Another one activated a trip flare while clearing the wire for the main body.

Albracht was sure the NVA would start firing at them instantly. But they caught a break. Everyone hit the ground, in the worst position possible: they were in the open with no concealment. They waited in the flare's light for NVA incoming fire. But, for some reason, none came their way. Something more welcome did: a Shadow.

Pierelli had an infrared strobe light that one of the Mike Force guys had given him months earlier when he was with his A-Team. By some stroke of luck, he still had it on Kate. The battery was low, but the light was still serviceable.

The sergeant turned on the light and asked the Shadow crew if they could see it. They could. Fortunately, Shadow was the only gun ship that had such infrared capabilities. Spooky did not.

Pierelli, always thinking ahead, left his infrared strobe light in the center of Kate as a reference point for Shadow. The plane used the light as a reference point for the layout of the hill and the E&E force's position. Pierelli and the Shadow crew spoke in meters for a better reference to enhance the chances of more precise cover fire from above. Once the troops departed from Kate, this light was a priceless beacon for Shadow.

With a Little Bit of Luck

The troops maintained their composure until the flare faded, even though it seemed like an eternity to them before it sputtered out. Then they resumed their withdrawal in a less-than-organized fashion. Once again, their progress was halted quickly.

They traveled only a short distance when the group stopped suddenly. Albracht worked his way to the point and learned that the CIDG point man had halted about twenty yards from the gap that separated Kate from Ambush Hill. He was just too scared to continue; Albracht assumed the point himself. That was not the ideal place for him, since the point man in any patrol was in danger of being hit first.

Even though the gunship was only minutes away, it was still too far out to fire into the gap and clear the troops' path. Again Albracht had to act immediately. There was no pulling back with the NVA right on their heels. Sounding like John Wayne—as well as the *Infantry Officer's Handbook*—he said, "Follow me!" He led the troops to and through the gap, with his radio operator right behind him.

Albracht remembered later that Tex carried his radio during the entire escape. "He was a large 'good old boy' cannonneer from Texas," the captain recalled, "and he was simply magnificent. He never faltered, never wavered, and always remained cool under fire." The kicker came later, however, when Tex admitted to Albracht that he suffered from night blindness.

Rogers stayed at Albracht's side throughout the E&E. They were separated only twice that night: once when Albracht went on a one-man recon patrol and again when he had to make contact with the Mike Force sent out to meet them. He was as reassuring on the ground as Spooky 41 was in the air.

The Radio Is Not Working

Rogers quickly demonstrated his skills as a radio operator—and a soldier—as soon as the E&E force moved off Kate.

Albracht called to Spooky on the radio, but there was no answer. He called again, with the same result: no answer. Impatiently, he tried a third time—and there was still no response. In frustration and anger, he turned to Rogers. "This damn radio isn't working!"

Tex looked at him and in a calm, amused, reassuring Southern drawl, and said, "Sir, you need to release the push-to-talk switch."

Albracht looked down at his hand and saw that he had the PTT (push-to-talk) switch depressed in a death grip. He released it—and Spooky came on the air immediately. The captain felt embarrassed, but he managed to mumble thanks to Tex, who was proving to be a major asset to the E&E group.

At that point, Albracht had an epiphany. He understood two things. First, he was as scared as everyone else. Second, he needed to remain calm and focused if he expected to get these troops through the night.

Down a Slippery Slope

Although the gap was a classic choke point for ambushes, they passed through it successfully. Albracht stayed in it moving the troops through until Sergeant Pierelli, whose assigned position was in the approximate middle, relieved him. Pierelli ensured that the troops stayed together and kept moving.

He and his rear guard were also responsible for covering the withdrawal. He exhibited his professionalism throughout the E&E and made it possible for Albracht to do what he had to do.

Albracht noted later that Pierelli was "Always calm, focused, and consummately professional, [and] made it possible for me to concentrate on my own mission at hand. Throughout the six days, Pierelli was my right-hand man, invaluable to the plan of defense and escape." His cool demeanor paid off at the gap.

The troops got down the north slope and through the gap in the wood line without much difficulty. So far, so good. But when they started up the next slope, the point men moved to the right of the hilltop, instead of to the left as they were supposed to. Albracht tried to steer them to the left, according to the plan. They ignored him and continued in the other direction. "They must know something I don't know," he thought. Albracht did not force the issue. He let them continue based on their familiarity with the area. His intuition and their knowledge paid off. But the unanticipated change in direction presented a new problem for Albracht.

In earlier clear radio traffic with Spooky and Shadow about their pending escape, Albracht had tried to ensure that the gunships knew their precise route, since they would fire their mini-guns ahead of the troops. His original plan had been to traverse to the left of the hill, and he did not expect to be in the gap. Nevertheless, there he was—and he was not in position to direct the point man.

Then again, he reasoned, if Spooky and Shadow did not arrive to provide support, the exact route no longer mattered anyway. By the time they moved out of the gap, Albracht reckoned, the main body was committed, so he accepted the move to the right. As a result, the E&Eers passed close enough to the top of Ambush Hill that if enemy were hiding in the darkness, they would not have seen them. But, if they had been there, and had moved, the E&E force would at least have heard them and been on them quickly. The whole issue was moot: the gunship was not on station anyway.

The column, still in a reasonable formation, skirted the hilltop, crossed the woodline where Albracht's point striker had been hit on October 29, and entered the thick, dark jungle. Then military decorum broke down. The troops became disoriented and disorganized. Albracht and Pierelli had to establish better order and discipline if the troops were going to survive the night.

The two leaders instructed the troops to go back to the edge of the wood line to reorganize. They were able to get about half of the troops headed away from Kate in a northerly direction by remaining at the jungle edge and making sure they followed the boots in front of them. Then, several men stepped out into the clearing at the edge of the wood line—and into a trap.

Ambush

An NVA .51-caliber machine-gun crew on top of the hill they had just skirted fired at them. Later, Albracht guessed that NVA personnel had been monitoring radio conversations concerning the withdrawal and determined that the firebase personnel would skirt that hill to the left, so they set up an ambush. Somehow the CIDG point men knew that and turned to the right. When they did, just behind the ambush site, the NVA could not shift their position without giving away their location. They had to wait until the E&E group reemerged in the clearing again to open fire. Whatever point it was, their ambush had the desired effect.

The green tracers of heavy machine-gun fire erupted just over the troops' heads. Initially uncertain of their origin, Albracht believed that Spooky and Shadow were firing on friendlies. He yelled, "Cease fire!" into the radio mike. The gunship crew told him that they were not firing—and weren't even on station yet. Then Albracht noticed that the fire was coming from the top of Ambush Hill.

Since the Spooky and Shadow crews were intimately familiar with that location, he asked them to "light it up" as soon as they got into position. Meanwhile, the rounds continued to go over the troops' heads at a dramatic rate of fire. Albracht determined the source of the firing.

Why was the .51-caliber, a tripod-mounted weapon, firing over their heads? he wondered. He guessed that due to the steepness of the hill whose bottom they occupied, the angle necessary for the weapon to engage them from the top of Ambush Hill was simply too great. He concluded that the gun was firing over their heads because of a combination of the height of the hill, the steep angle that the E&E force was in, and, above all, luck. Nor did he rule out divine intervention. In truth, he did not care about the *why*. As long as his troops were not being hit—that was all that mattered.

Eating Dirt

Everyone hit the ground to avoid being seen. They might as well have sat by a bonfire and waved a sign to the NVA saying, "Here we are," because they were lying on open ground in plain sight with orders not to return fire.

"We were told that if the enemy opened fire, don't return fire right away," Koon recalled. As Albracht explained to them, the enemy may just be "reconning by fire to figure out our location." At least one soldier defied the order and opened up with his M16, much to Koon's chagrin. "The trooper exposed us and burned my forearm with his muzzle flash when he laid the barrel across my arm," Koon said. "Fortunately for us, I don't think the enemy firing the machine gun could get the barrel low enough to hit us."

Despite its ineffectiveness, the fire caused the troops who had not entered the jungle yet to panic and begin crashing pell-mell through the brush. That was the last place Albracht wanted them to go. The darkness and the dense undergrowth would interfere with their ability to stay together, which would lessen their chances of escaping and evading the enemy. He and Pierelli tried unsuccessfully to stop them.

Albracht yelled for them to continue north as he raced ahead to take the lead of the main body. Along the way, he grabbed every trooper he could and pushed them in the direction of the column. Pierelli was doing the same in the rear while maintaining a security squad to cover the withdrawal. The chaos during the ambush was particularly upsetting for Johnson. He lost his eyeglasses. "I was already ten to twenty yards up the hill away from the wood line when the firing started," he said. "When I dove for the ground my eyeglasses fell off and were lost. I rolled and scooted back down the hill into the safety of the wood line. It was now nighttime. Under the triple-canopy jungle, it was pitch-black. Without my glasses (20/400 vision), I was essentially blind for the rest of the night." So was everyone else for all practical purposes.

Pitch-Blackness and Utter Confusion

As the troops reached the tree line, the sky was pitch-dark. Soldiers were falling into bomb craters left from the previous days' air strikes and yelling to one another in an attempt to link with everyone. It was very difficult for anyone to see more than a foot ahead.

Ten or fifteen minutes into the evacuation, Pierelli heard someone call, "Sarge!" He went forward to see what was wrong. The caller said he had broke off from the main column and was lost. This was a tough predicament for Pierelli—and everyone else.

He guided the missing soldier back to the main group and stressed that they needed complete silence. Once everyone shut up, he listened to what was going on around them. Because noise travels well at night, he was able to hear the other part of the column up ahead. Pierelli took the lead and instructed everyone to hold on to the web gear of the person in front of him, and under no conditions to let go. At that point, Albracht, separated from the rest of his force, resorted to Plan B.

Albracht instructed his troops to move out. Their progress was slow and fraught with tension. Finally, Spooky arrived on station and began ripping up the terrain on Ambush Hill and Kate, which was entirely in the hands of the NVA by that point. First, Spooky (call sign 41) had to resolve its position with Spad (Spad Zero Two) and coordinate with Albracht, whose call sign was Chickenhawk (CH).

Spooky Arrives

There was a bit of uncertainty between the pilots about whether one of them should drop a flare to get a better view of the terrain. Albracht settled the issue: no one should.

CH: Unintelligible . . . we're going out buddy, we're going out.

Understandably, Albracht sounded excited, and the Spad crew tried to settle him down.

Spad Zero Two: OK, Hawk, this is Spad. You're going to have to talk slower if you want these people to talk to you.

Spooky jumped in and assumed control of the situation.

41: Hey Spad, 41, stand by just one second. Listen (unintelligible). . . circling at Eight Thousand Five Hundred right above them. . . you can see it out your window they're taking incoming and the (unintelligible) is on the other side. Tell them to move out and we'll go down. Spad Zero Two, Spooky 41 is in orbit above you now, and if you move out, we'll go down and get the situation under control if we can, over.

That gave Albracht a quick shot of confidence, especially when Spooky reassured him with a few words of advice and a request for a location.

41: Hey there Chickenhawk, take it easy there my friend. We're right here, we're coming in right now. What's your sitch [situation]?

CH: [Unintelligible] . . . the tree line, coming down the valley.

41: Roger, roger, you're down in the tree lines in the valley in the northwest of the figure eight down there, is that affirmative?

CH: OK, listen, OK you're going to have to hold up on that. Our people are getting a little bit ahead of me.

Albracht began multitasking as he tried to coordinate the plane in the air and the troops on the ground. He told the men closest to him to stop in a clearing ahead. Once they did, they waited for the rest of the troops to join them. When no one did immediately, Albracht had a sinking feeling.

His spirits were soon lifted when he received a report that all the American personnel from the 5th Battalion, 22nd Artillery, were present, along with twenty or thirty CIDG soldiers. That turned out to be incorrect. Two U.S. artillerymen, along with a group of CIDG troops, were actually missing. One of them, Michael Robert Norton, never returned. The breakaway group, including the other missing artilleryman, somehow made it safely back to Buprang on their own.

One Man Missing

Aviators conducted aerial searches of the LZ and surrounding areas in an attempt to find Norton. They did not have any success. He was therefore classified as Missing in Action (MIA). His family waited patiently for the war to end, as did most of America. No one ever told them that he had been captured, so they waited and hoped for the best.

When the war ended, 591 American POWs were released from communist prison camps in Southeast Asia. Norton was not among them. Military authorities at the time were upset that such a small number of POWs had been released. They expected a much larger number. But, the North Vietnamese denied having anyone other than those 591 in their possession.

Lattin was the Quang Duc ALO when Norton disappeared. "We were flying in support of Kate for about ten days," he noted. "It was under heavy fire. During the night of 1–2 November is when Norton was lost. At that time the NVA did not attempt to keep anyone captured." That spelled doom for Norton.

Meanwhile, Pierelli's group walked, stopped, listened, walked, stopped, listened . . . after about twenty minutes or so, the splinter group hooked up with the main column. Albracht and Pierelli had finally restored some semblance of organization, but it was still so dark that each man had to hold on to the web gear of the man in front of him as they moved on.

Chapter 19

Confusion
Reigns in the Skies

*"Confusion heard his voice, and wild uproar Stood ruled, stood
vast infinitude confined; Till at his second bidding darkness fled,
Light shone, and order from disorder sprung."*

—JOHN MILTON

The ground-to-air transmissions the night of the E&E highlighted
the palpable confusion that affected the operation. Albracht's
excitement was apparent as he led the troops off the hill toward their
linkup with Mike Force. Various support personnel in the air and on
the ground tried as best they could to ease his excitement at times. But
they were not the ones worrying about incoming fire from the NVA
and other sources Albracht could not determine.

No one seemed to be in complete control as the E&E force moved
off the hill. With so many people on the radio, it was amazing that the
operation ran as smoothly as it did. At times it seemed as if there were
too many planes in the air. Even the NVA seemed confused at the
events that unfolded as the night wore on.

There were a few new players involved in the transmissions as
Albracht (call sign Chickenhawk) and his force moved toward their
Mike Force linkup. In the following transmission, Spooky 41 is U.S.
Air Force Captain Wells, the navigator on Spooky 41 the night of the

E&E. Carbon Outlaw 25 gave clearance for overall operations, scheduling replacement Spookys, and authorizing firing clearances for support units. Spad Zero Two is the Skyraider flying ground support over Kate. Lima Salines is Mike Force. These voices' presence was indicative of the intense morale and physical support available to Kate's defenders from soldiers and airmen who had no direct involvement in the fight, but who vowed to do all they could to save their buddies whose lives were in the balance.

The transmissions begin just about the time the E&E operation starts.

Unknown Station: Tell them we're circling right eight thousand five hundred right above them . . .

Unknown Station: That's a lot of shit out . . .

Unknown Station: . . . understand we'll be cleared to drop flares right above . . .

41: Okay, Chickenhawk, calm down. Get your information down there and just pass that up to me and we'll help you out, my friend.

CH: (Unintelligible) . . . hold your fire, hold your fire.

41: Spad, Spook 41, go.

Spad: Roger, they're moving from the firebase, to the north about 800 meters. You can just watch it here about for a few minutes and see where those lume (illumination) mortars are coming from—and they're not friendly.

41: Okay, understand those lume mortars are not friendly, right?

Spad: That's affirmative. They're from the bad guys.

41: Okay. Now, who's moving the 200 meters to the north, the good guys?

Spad: The good guys are to the north, that's affirmative.

41: Thank you much. (Internal: Okay, Lloyd [unintelligible] . . . keep them behind us. Tell them I'm going to get down in front of them, keep me in sight, I'm going down to fifteen hundred . . . Internal 2: . . . [unintelligible] . . . behind you, right? Internal: Got two airplanes behind me . . . too God damn many planes . . . for us to . . .)*

41: Roger, Spooky 41, we're descending to seven thousand.

Unknown Station: (Unintelligible) . . . we and a couple of other aircraft out here . . . (unintelligible) and the other is Zero Two. We're going to start dropping down to fifty-five hundred here, appreciate it if you'd keep an eye on us so we can both get down there.

Unknown Station: Thank you much.

41: Chickenhawk, 41, go ahead my friend.

CH: (Unintelligible) . . . one of our people popped a trip flare . . . (unintelligible)

41: Chickenhawk, you'll have to talk a little slower, take it easy, work with me up here. Now what's your situation, go ahead.

---

* Multiple stations transmitting at same time—too numerous to decipher individual stations accurately. Best estimation is that 41 is trying to get control to clear out some of the stations.

CH: Okay, buddy. One of our people (unintelligible).

41: (Internal: Roger, roger, have a flare at my nine o'clock position at this time.)

CH: Okay, a ground flare to our north, over.

41: Roger, flare to your north, we're looking now . . .

CH: Okay, buddy, why don't we put it to the north to the tree line, in the tree line . . . move this strobe, over.

41: I understand you want us to start working to the north, with that flare up into the tree line, is that right?

CH: Roger, right to the front, right to the north of the tree line, right there in the valley.

41: Okay. and ahh, Four One Zero to drop its own flares

CH: Okay, okay . . . ahead of me, my people . . . got ahead of me.

Spad: 41, this is Spad, target . . .

CH: Spooky, Spooky, this is the Hawk.

41: Roger, Hawk, Spook 41.

CH: Okay, my people got ahead of me a little bit, they're moving out.

41: Okay, real fine. Is 41 cleared to drop light, Chickenhawk?

Spad: Negative 41, this is Zero Two, hold the light. Hold the light.

41: Roger, Zero Two, 41 to hold. Hey, Hawk, understand you're moving out now. Is that affirmative? (Pilot, do you have that ground flare identified? Pilot: Yep. 41: Okay, very fine. Can you take it a hundred meters or two hundred meters to the north to the tree line?)

CH: That's affirmative, buddy, that's affirmative.

41: Okay, good deal. How about moving on down . . . (unintelligible) (41: Okay, we'll need our own light to get that . . .)

CH: . . . affirmative, affirmative, that's what we're doing.

Unknown Station: Spooky, hold on here a minute

41: Roger, we're ready whenever you are. (41: Okay, let's let these guys start moving, we don't want . . .)

CH: . . . moving out . . .

41: All right, we're up here ready when you get your men in position and out of the way. We're going to roll in and give you a hand.

CH: Okay, buddy. We'll keep our heads down, but don't fire to the north, the north, okay?

41: Roger, we understand. We won't be firing to the north. You want us to stay to the east in that valley down there in the draw down there, right?

CH: (Whispering) Roger. Hey, we're down at the bottom now and our people are moving out real fine, no trouble so far, WHOA . . . operator, no sweat.

41: Take it easy down there, Hawk.

CH: No trouble so far, no trouble so far. (Whispering) I'll keep you posted.

41: . . . moving north . . . November . . . moving north . . .

Unknown Station: Roger, roger, understand, we'll stay to the south. We'll be working the eastern and southeastern portions.

41: (41: Now I think what we'll need to do once we get our light out we won't have any trouble marking the area. Internal: [Unintelligible] 41: I'd like to get that light out as soon as possible. . . radio . . . drop our flares.)

CH: (Whispering and out of breath) Pretty good. Hello, Hawk to control, we're moving pretty good.

Kangaroo Control: Roger that, let me know when you come across that first bald hill and starting down this way, over.

CH: Correction, buddy. We're by Ambush Hill. We're going up on the left side, the left side.

Kangaroo Control: Roger that. When you come across that hill and start down into this next wood line you'll be coming into me, over.

CH: (Whispering) Roger on that.

41: Chickenhawk, Spooky 41.

CH: Spooky 41. Hey, buddy, what's happening?

41: Just want to keep in contact with you down here. I'm seeing if we can drop our flares, my friend. Chickenhawk, 41, do you read me?

CH: (Whispering) Hey, buddy, give me about One Zero minutes.

41: Roger, Chickenhawk.

Kangaroo Control: Hey, Spooky 41 . . .

41: Roger, Kangaroo Control, 41, read you Five By.

Kangaroo Control: Roger, appreciate it if no flares are dropped on until you get an all clear from me. I got four different elements out there . . . en route . . . get these people in and I'm controlling from here. When they're clear and linked up and on their way to mission, then we'll let it go from there. But let me do it from here and not on the ground, over.

41: Roger, I'll coordinate with you, Kangaroo Control.

Kangaroo Control: Fine, I'll be finished with this element here about 500 meters to the northwest . . . runs east west . . . and grab any Viking, any Viking is the next call sign you'll pick up with . . . any Viking . . .

CH: Lima Salines, Lima Salines, this is Chickenhawk, over.

Lima Salines: This is Lima Salines, over.

CH: (Whispering) We got . . . on top of the hill and we'll be coming down the hill into your location.

Shadow 48: 41, Shadow 48.

41: Roger, Shadow 48, go.

Shadow 48: We're going to be coming in over the . . . we're at Eight point Five . . .

41: Roger, roger, 41 is at Five Five now.

Lima Salines: Chickenhawk, this is Lima, roger that. My people have been notified of this type movement . . . over.

CH: (Whispering) Okay, buddy. Right now pushing to top of the hill by the blown-out wooded area.

Lima Salines: I am not, I repeat, I am not at the location that was given to me, over.

41: Zero Two, Spooky 41.

Spad: 41, Zero Two.

41: Zero Two . . . contact with Carbon Outlaw. They want to know the name of the ground commander that was controlling the air strike. Do you know who it was?

Spad: No, I don't think, should be able to get that . . . It was Chickenhawk that was . . . the air strike.

41: Okay, Chickenhawk, we're going to have to drop light before we can . . . Break, Break, Kangaroo Control, Spooky 41.

CH: Okay.

41: Chickenhawk, hold on, stand by one. Let me contact Kangaroo Control down here. Kangaroo Control, Spooky 41.

Kangaroo Control: Spooky 41, this is Kangaroo Control . . . negative at this time. I'll give you the word from here when we want you to . . .

41: Roger, Kangaroo Control. Break, break Chickenhawk, hold on my friend. Got to get the complete clearance from Kangaroo Control and then we'll hit it. Chickenhawk, 41, you copy?

CH: (Loud breathing)

Kangaroo Control: Roger, Spooky 41. Could you call Lima Salines and see if the linkup is complete and also have him relay to me . . . his location . . . over.

41: Roger, roger. Break, Lima Salines, Lima Salines from 41.

Lima Salines: Spooky 41, this is Lima Salines. Be advised, we still haven't linked up here, we'll give you a call when we do, over.

41: Roger. We'd like to know ASAP as soon as you link up so we can get started up here.

Lima: Roger that, buddy, I'll let you know as soon as possible.

41: Roger, Break Kangaroo, 41, did you copy?

Kangaroo Control: This is Kangaroo . . .

CH: Lima, this is Chickenhawk, this is Chickenhawk.

Lima Salines: Salines, over.

CH: Okay, buddy, we're coming into you now. Look, I'm getting them into a single file. It's a long one, but you're only gonna have one entrance into your perimeter, only one entrance into your perimeter, only one people coming in one line. I'm trying to . . . hope it don't get screwed up by the time it gets down to you, you roger?

Lima Salines: Roger that, come on in. I'll let my people know.

CH: Roger, roger. Okay, we're moving in now . . . they might be hitting your perimeter now, it'll be a big long line, but don't worry, buddy (whispering). We only got one line coming in.

41: Kangaroo Control, you copy Lima Salines?

Kangaroo Control: Negative, I can't read them.

41: Roger, Lima Salines, you have to link up on rebounding tone and Chickenhawk, they're just about ready to let us know as soon as they got the linkup.

Lima Salines: Roger, I'll be standing by.

41: Roger, roger, I'll let you know.

Lima Salines: Lima Salines, it's not complete yet, over.

41: Roger, roger, keep us posted, my friend.

Lima Salines: Roger, will do.

Unknown Station: Can you hear Chickenhawk . . .

41: Haven't heard from him in a little while, I've been monitoring. Break, Chickenhawk, Spooky 41.

CH: Okay. Spooky 41, this the Hawk here. I'd like to contact Lima Salines, over.

41: Lima Salines, this is Spooky 41. Chickenhawk is trying to contact you.

Lima Salines: Roger, Chickenhawk, this is Lima Salines, over.

CH: Okay. Listen, here's what we're gonna do. We got in the wrong path here a little bit, so we're pulling back up to the wood line instead of this jungle. I am going to be at the north end, north end, and when I get up there and get my people there, could you send us a small party of two or three people out to the wood line and walk to the north and you can link up with us and lead us back to your perimeter, over.

41: Roger, roger, is this Chickenhawk calling 41?

CH: Roger, roger. Chickenhawk calling 41, Chickenhawk calling 41.

41: Roger, Chickenhawk. Calm down, my friend. 41, go ahead.

CH: Okay, buddy. Somebody's firing on us up there.

41: (Internal: Okay. Ask him if he's firing at us and we're clear to fire back at them.) Okay, Chickenhawk, is this man firing at us or at you, my friend?

CH: Okay, buddy, he's firing at me, he's firing at me. What other aircraft is up there?

41: Okay, all aircraft, attention all aircraft, cease fire, cease fire, you're firing on Chickenhawk's position.

Shadow 48: Shadow 48, we are not firing.

41: Spooky 41 is not firing. Chickenhawk, are you sure you took any fire from above?

CH: Okay, buddy . . . down in this hole and it looked like it was firing on my people from above. I'm gonna get a real close look and I'll let you know, okay?

41: Okay, Chickenhawk. Just take it easy, my friend, now.

Lima Salines: Hawk to his north . . .

41: Roger, roger, Break, Hawk, 41, Lima Salines is calling and wants you to move to your north, move to your north. Chickenhawk, Chickenhawk, Spooky 41, did you copy? Contact with Lima Salines.

Kangaroo Control: Roger, Okay. Push . . . down here . . . relay and . . . hear Lima Salines, over.

41: Roger, roger, I'll relay anything you need.

Lima Salines: Hawk, this is Lima Salines, over.

Spad: . . . handle this thing. We'd like to return to base now . . . Shadow . . . so that we can get back out here early in the morning.

41: Roger, roger, 41, as soon as they can give us clearance to pop flares and stuff we can keep it under control.

Spad: We're just kind of spinning our wheels right now staying out of the way, and if we can go back right now we can get an early start in the morning.

41: Roger, Zero Two, thanks much for your assistance. Go ahead and get some good sleep.

Kangaroo Control: Zero Two, Zero Two, this is Kangaroo, over.

Spad: Roger . . .

41: Kangaroo Control, Spooky 41. Okay, Control . . . bit quieter now. How about giving me a rundown and see if we can pinpoint the exact area where you're gonna want us to go in and fire if we can so we can get started as soon after we drop light as possible.

Kangaroo Control: Wait one.

CH: This is Chickenhawk, this is Chickenhawk. Anybody want me?

41: Ahh, Chickenhawk, this is 41. I'm talking to Kangaroo Control. How's things going with you, my friend?

CH: Oh, a little bit rugged, my friend. This . . . I'll tell you right now is hell. (Breathing hard). I'll tell you. But ahh . . .

Chapter 20

Linkup

*"Always give a word or sign of salute when meeting or passing
a friend, or even a stranger, if in a lonely place."*

—TECUMSEH

Albracht and the gunship maintained a continual conversation. The
last thing the captain wanted Spooky to do was place covering
fire anywhere near his position. He made it abundantly clear to Spooky
that they were heading north. Worse, the planes were getting in one
another's way, and the NVA was illuminating the area in an effort to
locate the E&E force.

Too many planes was not a problem for Albracht. But, the fear
that one or more of them might fire in his direction was. He could
only maintain contact with Spooky and keep his troops moving.

There Is Nothing Worse than Waiting

The E&E goal was still to link up with Mike Force. But after the mad
dash away from the hostile Ambush Hill fire, Albracht was still not
sure where he and his troops were or where Mike Force was. He kept

moving the troops in the direction where he felt the Mike Force might be in order to put distance between them and the NVA.

He explained to everyone that they had to travel silently along a circuitous route to the designated rendezvous site with the relief troops who had established a defensive position two miles away. It was not feasible for Mike Force to move closer to LZ Kate. Albracht reinforced the message to his troops coolly and with determination that he would lead them to the linkup with Mike Force. But, he warned, if any NVA troops located them, the rest of their large force would converge quickly on their location and disrupt the linkup. With that caveat in mind, the troops set off to find the relief force.

The force continued to move very carefully and quietly though the jungle for about five more hours toward their rendezvous with Mike Force, maintaining their cover all the way. Albracht halted their movement more than once because he heard sounds nearby. Each time he took it upon himself to investigate. At one point he heard movement in the darkness about 100 yards to his immediate left and ordered everyone to get down. There was a large body of troops moving in the opposite direction parallel to the E&E force.

The captain radioed Mike Force in hushed tones and informed them that if they were moving, his troops were on their immediate left. The answer did not surprise him. They reported that they were not moving. It became apparent to Albracht that the troops on the move were NVA.

All the E&E force could do was wait for them to pass as they lay quietly on the jungle floor within earshot of the enemy. It was a long and scary time for them, but the NVA force eventually moved on. Once they did, the troops continued on their route through the triple-canopy jungle in almost total darkness, trying to maintain stealth. Moving even a small group with stealth in such terrain is agonizingly slow and difficult—and virtually impossible with a large group. Yet, they progressed slowly and with purpose. Their lives hung in the balance.

As the troops approached a clearing, Albracht told them to wait quietly. The clearing, about 110 yards wide, was completely flat and covered with waist-high grass. Albracht heard a single muffled clanking sound on the far side. He realized that there were soldiers there, but were they Mike Force or NVA?

Who Is It?

Albracht analyzed the situation quickly. All he knew for certain was that this flat clearing with its border of dense trees was the perfect place for the NVA to have set up a new kill zone. To enter the clearing blindly could mean swift and certain death for his column, especially if they were suddenly illuminated by an enemy flare or by moonlight breaking through the clouds. Even signaling silently with his red-filtered flashlight from this present position could easily bring on enemy fire.

Speaking very quietly, the captain radioed his position to the Mike Force, describing terrain features instead of map coordinates in case the North Vietnamese were intercepting his communications. He asked them to send a man forward into the clearing. But the Mike Force, understandably acting with extreme caution in case they were being tempted by an NVA ruse, instructed him to send a man forward instead. "The relief troops should be waiting in the wood line on the other side of the clearing," he said quietly to the nearest soldiers. "It's extremely dangerous to approach friendly units at night under these circumstances. Therefore, we must remain in place and keep still." By "we," he meant his troops.

After a short wait, Albracht told Lieutenant Smith and Sergeant Pierelli that he wanted to go out ahead by himself to see if he could pinpoint the E&E force's exact location on the map, using terrain features. Albracht told them that when they challenged him upon his return he would signal with two short flashes from the red-filtered flashlight he carried. Truthfully, he was not sure he would return at all.

Albracht Puts His Life on the Line—Again

Because the enemy was combing the jungle for the E&E group, there was a distinct possibility that Albracht could be captured. With that in mind, he delivered his final instructions: if he did not flash twice, they were to presume that he had been compromised—and they were to open fire. It almost came to that.

Albracht went out about 100 yards from the E&E group, but he could not get a definite fix on their position. While moving, he tripped over the root of a tree in the dark and fell flat on his face after brushing against the branches. As he checked himself out, he realized that the red-filtered flashlight he carried clipped to his load-bearing suspenders was missing.

The captain felt along the ground in the darkness, but he could not find the flashlight. He crawled from the base of the tree in bigger and bigger circles. Still no flashlight. Without it, he would not be able to re-enter his own lines. The flashlight code had no fail-safe. No light, no re-entry.

For once his composure flagged. Fighting off mild panic, he began at the base of the tree trunk and slowly felt his way up to its limbs. Success! There, snagged on a small branch by its clip, was his flashlight. He decided that he had experienced enough of his one-man reconnaissance and returned hurriedly to his troops—but not for long.

Another Trip into the Unknown

It was time for another one-man recon. Albracht told Pierelli, Smith, and Rogers to stay put with the men while he attempted to make physical contact with Mike Force. He had radioed Mike Force and told them that he believed they were in close proximity and would be attempting to make contact. But, because of the darkness, enemy movement, and unclear terrain features at night, he just didn't know for sure where he was, nor did the Mike Force know his location with certainty.

Albracht's last instructions to Pierelli and Smith were simple: if this was in fact an NVA position instead of Mike Force, they should forget about him and just move the troops on quietly and quickly in a northwest direction to Buprang, since the NVA may not have known yet that there were others with him.

The captain started across the open field, talking in a normal conversational voice. "I am an American. Are you the Mike Force?" NVA troops were everywhere, and for all Albracht knew he was walking into one of their encampments. He repeated his questions several times as he got closer to the wood line.

Halle-Lowell-jah

To Albracht's dismay, nobody acknowledged his presence immediately. For security reasons, Mike Force could not acknowledge him as he crossed the open field because they could not be certain that he had not been captured and compromised. Then he broke into the wood line and looked down to see a Mike Force striker in a foxhole looking back at him.

Sergeant First Class Lowell Stevens, the Mike Force ground commander, grabbed Albracht's arm and told him to hurry and get the rest of his troops, since the NVA were everywhere and they had to evacuate immediately. Three klicks and five hours after the E&E force had left Kate, they were linked up with their rescue force.

Albracht breathed a sigh of relief, ran back, contacted the troops, and prepared to move everyone out. He guided them across the clearing to the foxholes of the relief troops. Some of the troops did not know immediately what was going on. Koon was among them. For him the linkup had some almost comic undertones. "I was toward the rear of the column and wasn't informed that we were entering the Mike Force perimeter," he related. "As I entered, I fell into a foxhole, staring at two armed Montagnard soldiers, one on my left and one on my right. I wasn't sure if they were friendly or NVA. Of course, I had to ask the stupid question, 'Are you friendly?' Of course they were. If they hadn't been, who knows how that would have ended."

Albracht had safely completed his linkup with the relief column, but his ordeal was far from over.

We Are Not out of the Woods Yet

Sergeant Stevens advised that there were vastly superior enemy forces in the area that had been moving outside their hidden perimeter during the night. He believed they had been primarily looking for the escapees from Kate. Therefore, he said—as if it were really necessary—they had to evacuate the area before they were all discovered.

It was approximately 3 A.M. on November 2—five hours after the E&E began. They had traveled about two and a half miles during that time. Time and distance aside, they were still not out of the woods, literally or figuratively.

The Mike Force advisors took command of the operation. The alignment of Mike Force and Kate personnel took only minutes to organize before the combined groups departed to rendezvous with the companies of the 1st Battalion, 2nd MSFC. Sergeant Stevens put one Mike Force company in the lead and one in the rear, with the Kate defenders in the middle. Even with their combined strength, the Mike Force and Kate personnel were no match for their pursuers if a battle began. They stepped off in silence toward safety—they hoped.

Their exodus continued for another ten hours in a slow and cautious pace on an evasive route. The leaders believed the NVA troops knew where they were heading and were trying to intercept and ambush them. Sergeant Stevens, a savvy combat veteran, was well aware of this and directed the combined force's movements accordingly.

They moved in a well-organized and synchronized operation as they passed through succeeding rendezvous positions. The companies of the 1st Battalion remained in their positions as a rear guard in case the enemy pursued the column. For some inexplicable reason, the NVA did not attempt to follow.

The Final Tally

The six-day nightmare at Kate was over. The defenders paid a price, as reflected in the official army casualty reports: U.S. Army aviation—four killed; U.S. Army artillery—two killed, six wounded, and one missing; U.S. Army Special Forces—two (slightly) wounded; CIDG CSF—four killed, seventeen wounded, and thirteen missing; CIDG MSF—one killed, seventeen wounded, and five missing.

The numbers only tell a part of the story. The human cost can never be tallied in numbers alone. There was a psychological cost as well, one that can never be measured. The action at Kate still haunts many of the people who served there in whatever capacity. They remember in particular their comrades who did not survive the ordeal. Their memories set in as they approached Buprang on November 2, 1969. For most of them, they continue to linger, for good or for bad.

Home at Last

Against all the odds, the E&E force marched into Buprang at 11 A.M. on November 2. The defenders of Kate had been moving continually through enemy territory in escape-and-evade mode for thirteen hours. Significantly, from the start of the actual E&E to the arrival back at Buprang, they had suffered only one casualty, plus the loss of Private Norton. Everything considered, it was a small miracle.

Captain Albracht captured the spirit of the escapade in his after-action report on the E&E:

> From October 28 through the escape on the evening and morning of November 1 and 2, it had been a living and unending perdition. As I reflect back on it, my memory becomes clearer, my senses keener, and I can almost smell the cordite in the air.
>
> I have never felt that I was needed more, nor have I ever been more scared. I was sent to do a specific mission, but a new and more important mission had suddenly and unexpectedly evolved—to lead these 150-odd souls to safety, since surrender was never an option.
>
> I did not volunteer for the assignment, but it was thrust upon me by circumstances. Once I realized exactly what fate

had charged me to do, no power in heaven or on Earth would prevent me from delivering these men out of harm's way—or I would die trying.

I truly do not know how we made it out that night. Although I do not dwell on it nowadays, it does come to mind more times than I care to admit. A smell, a sound, a turn of phrase, and I can be right back there again. It had an everlasting impact on my life and soul.

Johnson had a satisfying feeling as they approached Buprang. He observed multiple jet fighter bombing runs upon Kate. They were destroying whatever was left there. And he enjoyed the return of his eyesight after daybreak when he pulled from his pocket his extra pair of dark prescription sunglasses that he had placed there before leaving the FDC bunker.

The glasses gave him a new view of life, just as Albracht's leadership had done for so many of the Kate survivors. While they rested, their counterparts at LZs Susan and Annie were just beginning their own extractions, albeit under less strenuous circumstances.

Chapter 21

Leaving
Susan and Annie

"I been a long time leaving,
but I'm going to be a long time gone."

—WILLIE NELSON

While Albracht and Pierelli planned their escape without much help from the outside, administrators away from Kate were busy formulating a strategy and tactics to evacuate LZs Susan and Annie. The troops at Susan received the news at 6 P.M. on November 1 that they would be leaving the base the next day. Similar information arrived at Annie four hours later. The news did not come as a surprise to anyone—especially the troops at Susan.

Captain Klaus Adam, the commanding officer for the units there, had been told beforehand that he and his troops would be leaving. And seventy-five new pieces of equipment to be used in an extraction arrived at Susan through supply channels on the afternoon of November 1. That was a sure sign that the base was scheduled for extraction. Annie had received thirty sets of air items. However, the final plans for the two extractions were still incomplete.

Detailed planning for the dual extractions took place between 6 P.M. on November 1 and 7 A.M. the next day. The move required precise plans, which were developed under the leadership of action officer Maj. R. C. Baldwin, assistant action officer Capt. Neil Laughy, Captain Adam, and Capt. James Kersey, his counterpart at Annie. (Kersey suffered the indignity of being wounded in the buttocks at Annie, where he was treated by medic "Doc" Hamilton.)

One of the keys to the extraction of all the firebases was the availability of aircraft. The fact that three of the bases were being extracted at once placed a strain on the amount of support available to them individually. The troops had to be supplied adequately for their E&Es and the guns had to be removed if possible. There was little hope that the guns could be removed from Kate, which was the most vulnerable of the three bases. Therefore, planners focused more on the operations at Susan and Annie.

Dispersing the Inventory

Wisely, the planners did not try to evacuate both Susan and Annie at once. The final plan called for the extraction of Susan to begin at first light on November 2. The operation at Annie was scheduled to start at noon. Major Baldwin went to Susan to oversee the operation there. Captain Laughy supervised the move at Annie. The troops, guns, and whatever else could be salvaged would be split between and among several locations.

All 155 Class V and Class IV supplies from Susan were destined for LZ Mike Smith. All 105 Class V was slated to go to Buprang. All other materiel and personnel there went to Ban Me Thuot. (Classes were classifications and subclasses of items. Samples of items included in various classes were: Class I, rations/food; Class II, individual weapons, boots, clothes, and so on; Class III, petroleum oil and lubricants; Class IV, barbed wire and construction material; Class V, ammunition and explosives, including small-arms ammo, grenades, and artillery ammo; Class VI, items that were not necessary.)

Personnel and materiel were to be divided between Buprang and Ban Me Thuot. Two 105s with their sections; FDC and their staff; all Class V, IV, and I supplies; and the troops' personal baggage were assigned to Buprang. The rest of the personnel and materiel would go to Ban Me Thuot. All personnel and materiel going to Ban Me Thuot would be staged through Nhon Co and then transported to Ban Me Thuot on C-130s. Everything was in place. The plan looked good on paper—as plans so often do. Implementing them smoothly was a different matter—as it often is.

The Best-Laid Schemes . . .

The operation at Susan began at 9 A.M., long after the troops at Kate had completed their successful E&E. Ten helicopters participated: eight hooks and two cranes. There was an element of haste involved. Administrators had intercepted several messages from the enemy alerting them to possible attacks on Susan.

As the troops at Susan listened to the sounds of chopping around their positions on the night of November 1, they were sure they were the NVA's new target. The defenders were ready to leave, lest they suffer the same fate as their friends at Kate. Their sense of relief was palpable as the extraction began.

The plan was based on the idea that all the aircraft involved would concentrate on the extraction of Susan until noon. After that, half of them would be diverted to Annie. Even though the extractions would be going on simultaneously, they would be two separate operations. In fact, they were conducted on two separate FM radio frequencies so they would not interfere with one another. Everything worked well at first.

By 11:45 A.M., most of the material had been removed from Susan without any difficulty. That pleased Major Baldwin, who oversaw the operation from Susan. Actually, he did not have a choice as to where he was positioned.

Normally, Baldwin had a slick at his disposal in case he had to move from place to place to address any problems that might develop with communications, air items, etc. That day, however, the ubiquitous Lieutenant Colonel Delaune had commandeered his chopper to use in and around Nhon Co and Ghia Nhia. Effectively, Baldwin was grounded, which was no problem as long as the extraction continued flawlessly. The inevitable snags developed, though.

About noon, just as the extraction of Annie was scheduled to begin, refueling problems surfaced at Nhon Co and Ghia Nhia, from which the choppers were operating. That slowed down the operations a bit.

Baldwin was not aware of the situation at first, since communications between Susan and the two chopper bases were poor. To make matters worse, the air force's staging operations out of Nhon Co were posing a problem. Baldwin, the Action Officer, was stuck at Susan without access to a chopper. Unknown to him, Laughy had one at Annie. That did not do Baldwin a bit of good.

All's Well That Ends Well

Despite Baldwin's feeling of helplessness and the delays in the process at Annie, the problems proved surmountable. Choppers continued to move in and out at Annie, as they did at Susan. Ironically, one of the more serious hang-ups occurred at Susan, where Baldwin was located.

Toward the end of the operation, troops discovered that they had neglected to move one load of miscellaneous Class V material. It did not have a "donut" attached, without which it could not be lifted by a chopper. They rectified the problem by loading the materiel internally on a chopper. That was not the ideal way to transport the load, but it sufficed.

The troops' ability to adapt, improvise, and overcome resolved a chaotic situation and put a satisfactory end to an otherwise smooth operation. The extraction was completed at 2:45 P.M., when the last load of personnel left the base. At that point, Delaune arrived at Susan and picked up Baldwin. They flew to Annie to check on the operation there. Everything was proceeding satisfactorily there. Delaune and Baldwin departed to check on a deadly ambush that had destroyed a couple choppers and then continued to Ban Me Thuot.

The extraction of Annie ended at 5:35 P.M. on November 2. It was uneventful, until the end, when the NVA launched an attack on the base that precipitated a rushed conclusion to the operation. Nevertheless, the overall results of the extraction were satisfactory—but costly. Colonel Bowers's prophesy that the firebases were meant to be temporary had proved to be true.

"The important thing is [that] the artillerymen on those three [firebases] had already done their job of supporting the troops," he said. "There wasn't any need for them any longer on the hills. The operations on the ground were completed. And these firebases would have been evacuated soon anyway. They were sitting ducks."

The troopers who had just escaped from Kate could attest to that.

The Scorecard

One load had to be destroyed at Annie because of the last-minute NVA attack. A second burned in a helicopter crash. A load from Susan had been dropped. The personnel and their howitzers scheduled to go to Ban Me Thuot were stranded temporarily at Buprang, although they did complete the trip the following morning.

Overall, the planners of the two extractions could be pleased with the final results. The operations were completed with limited planning time and within strict time parameters. The planners were well aware that if they did not complete the extractions by the evening of November 2, the bases would suffer the same fate as Kate. They wanted to avoid that outcome at all costs. They did—and they learned some valuable lessons in the process.

The problems that arose during the extractions were solvable. The major difficulties included a shortage of fuel at the refueling points, a lack of experience in coordination between U.S. Army and U.S. Air Force personnel regarding the C-130 move from Nhon Co to Ban Me Thuot, poor communications at Annie caused by jammed frequencies and Vietnamese usurpation of the airways, and the sudden attack at the end of the operation. It took two days, but the planners developed solutions to the problems that could be implemented to forestall them in future operations.

Most importantly, the personnel from Susan and Kate were out of harm's way at more secure locations. That was the ultimate goal of the operation, just as it had been at Kate. The extraction methods were a bit different, but the outcomes were the same. Scores of young soldiers had lived to fight another day, go home—or both.

Chapter 22

Mayhem
and Medals

*"A leader is a man who can adapt
principles to circumstances."*

—GENERAL GEORGE S. PATTON

The troops got back to Buprang and resumed their military lives.
The army is not known for saying, "Thanks for an extraordinary
effort. Take a few days off," after soldiers complete a successful mission. Kate was an exception—after a few reflections, many thanks, and
a little excitement.

Enough Thanks to Go Around

Pierelli was profuse in his thanks for the people from different
branches of the U.S. armed forces who had made their E&E possible.
He was especially effusive in his praise for Maj. George Lattin, the
FAC who had supported the firebase and directed the F-100 Super
Sabers and older SPADs that conducted the air strikes on the enemy
positions during the day.

Pierelli concluded frankly, "Aviation saved our asses on the base.
The air force pounded the shit out of the enemy with strafing,

500-pounders, and napalm. The LOH and Huey gunships did a great job also. B-52s struck, too, but they were way off in the distance and not too close. The NVA took heavy casualties."

He was particularly thankful for the Spooky and Shadow pilots who provided cover on the night of the E&E. "The night we left, as it was described to me later, Spooky and Shadow circled and gave bursts with their mini-guns all night to give the impression people still were on the hill. The next morning F-4 Phantoms came and dropped 2,000-pounders and destroyed everything left there. That was the report we got. Also, as we were making our way back to Buprang with the Mike Force leading us, there were friendly artillery rounds coming over us and being fired behind us in the event that we were being followed. That is what we were told by the Aussies, if I remember correctly."

Pierelli was correct in his assessment of the F-4 Phantoms' raids on Kate to destroy the guns. One helicopter pilot was not too happy about being ordered to fly over Kate to verify what happened to the guns after the F-4s ended their runs.

Checking the Guns

One of the first things the brass at Buprang wanted to do was make sure the guns left behind on Kate were truly out of commission. Helicopter pilot Todd M. Petersen was unlucky enough to draw the assignment to fly over the base. It was hardly the highlight of his tour at the time.

Petersen was a slick aircraft commander. As he recalled, "My most vivid memory was my trip to Kate with the artillery commander the day after it was overrun. I seem to remember that he was an O-6 (colonel) and that I picked him up in Ban Me Thuot and flew him out to Kate. There were four or five passengers, so I guess they were part of his staff or maybe a Special Forces guy or two." The colonel wanted to verify what had happened to the guns. "As we headed to Kate, we located the artillerymen and the CIDG group making their way on the ground back to Buprang. They were pretty strung out, more so than I would have expected. The terrain was hilly with alternating open areas and thick forest. I remember thinking that they were very exposed.

"We proceeded to Kate," Petersen said. "I was very concerned about the NVA's .51-caliber guns and was trying to stay at least 3,000 feet above ground level," That did not make the colonel happy. He wanted to get much lower. "We had a bit of a pissing contest over the issue," Petersen remembered. "I did get a bit lower but the colonel was not happy. I wasn't too concerned about his opinion, as we could clearly see the gun pits. I think they were 105s. One gun was still in its pit. Another was turned up on its side and we were not able to locate the third gun. That was one of the reasons the colonel was pissed at me."

Again Petersen was not sympathetic to the colonel's desires. "I still didn't think getting any lower was going to make a difference and I didn't do it. An Air Force FAC showed up and instructed us to move off to the west as some F-4s were going to come in and try to destroy the guns. We settled in for the show."

According to Petersen, on the second or so bombing run, one of the "fast movers" took some kind of antiaircraft fire. The FAC thought it was a 37mm or a 57mm and that it came from that little tip of Cambodia sticking down into Vietnam to the north. That concerned Petersen. "I didn't know if they could shoot that far, but that gun could have taken us out in no time. But it was waiting for bigger game apparently." He left the area quickly and took the passengers back to Buprang. That marked the end of Petersen's involvement with Kate, but the troops who had escaped were in for an unsettling reminder.

Out of the Firing Pan, Into the Fire

After the troopers arrived at Buprang, they expressed their joy at making it through the ordeal. They were running on pure adrenaline and needed to crash. Albracht provided a quick debriefing and went straight to his bunk, where sleep overtook him immediately. He noted that if he dreamed anything at all, he could not remember what it was. What he did remember was the sudden, loud sound of incoming mortars and recoilless rifle rounds.

It was late in the evening of November 2; Buprang, the place where Albracht and his troops thought they were safe—at least safer than Kate—was under attack. Everyone on Special Forces Team A-236 had an assigned position; his was the .50-caliber machine gun mounted on top of a bunker at the apex of the camp perimeter.

Albracht took up his post and immediately spotted the location of the recoilless rifle, just within the range of his machine gun. He put the rifle under fire, using tracers to walk his rounds into the location. The duel accelerated.

The captain's first rounds got the recoilless rifleman's attention. The NVA soldier's next round was aimed directly at Albracht, but it landed at the base of his position. The explosion knocked him out of the elevated bunker, but he climbed back up and returned an intense stream of fire.

The tail of fire from the NVA rifleman's next round appeared to be coming directly at Albracht's machine gun. This time he jumped voluntarily to the ground. The explosive impact was close—very close. Albracht once again mounted the bunker, righted the overturned .50, and poured a stream of direct fire onto the enemy. Although the NVA gunner managed to get off two more rounds in rapid succession, they were wild and exploded harmlessly short of the bunker. Albracht continued to rake the entire position until it was silent.

By that time, the captain's machine gun was overheated and needed to cool. But the base was now receiving B-40 rockets in addition to everything else. Albracht immediately contacted the Spooky and Shadow gunships that had arrived on station.

Spooky and Shadow, Come on Down!

Coolly, they held a brief reunion. Then, Albracht directed fire on the rocket positions. To do so, he had to move to an exposed position to effectively identify and eliminate the fire. Once he was there, Albracht pinpointed the enemy positions and vectored the mini-guns in.

All incoming ceased once Spooky and Shadow unleashed their particular version of hell onto the positions. The battle ended as quickly as it began, and Albracht was free to enjoy a combat- and stress-free environment, at least temporarily. He could concentrate on mundane matters for a while.

Medals for Everyone—except Albracht

There were medals to be distributed, in-country R&R to be taken, reunions to be held, and new assignments to be made. One of those reunions was between Kenn Hopkins and his comrades, which highlighted the bonds between and among soldiers who are involved in precarious situations.

Hopkins reconnected with his artillerymen once he got back to Ban Me Thuot, where he was debriefed and sent to the rest of the Charlie Battery, which was already there. He did not know how they would receive him. "After the LZ was evacuated and the guys were brought back to Charlie Battery, I reluctantly went to see the guys I left on LZ Kate," he said. "I was surprised and relieved when they came up to me asking where I had gone; some thought I was left there. There was no hate or discontent with my leaving them. That night we watched a movie and talked about our experiences on Kate and what happened after I left the LZ and their walk to Buprang."

Another housekeeping task was the awards ceremony that took place at Ban Me Thuot on November 13, 1969, to recognize the survivors of Kate for their bravery. Colonel Hall, the commanding officer of IFFV, visited Battery C 1/92d Artillery at Ban Me Thuot to present awards for the troops' heroism at Kate. The list of decorations was impressive. One name was missing: Capt. William L. Albracht.

Granted, Albracht was not a member of the artillery unit, and according to the unit's Operational Reports/Lessons Learned account for November 1, 1969, to January 31, 1970, nothing extraordinary had happened at Kate. It read simply: "At the beginning of the reporting period, Battery C (-) was at Buprang (YU495558) and Btry C (Plt) was at LZ Kate (YU581548) on 2 Nov 69, Btry C (Plt) moved by foot from LZ Kate to Buprang (YU495558). Both 155mm howitzers were destroyed at LZ Kate so move involved only personnel." The report was just one more in a string of reports that made the exit from Kate sound like a family's Sunday stroll along an oceanfront pier.

Nevertheless, Brockwell was incredulous when he learned that Albracht had not received a medal. In May 2011 he wrote a letter supporting a Medal of Honor for Albracht, "I was aware at the time that several of the artillerymen and the Special Forces personnel were receiving awards for valor in what we termed an 'impact award' ceremony. [An impact award is given shortly after an action but before the paperwork goes in.] I did not find out until years later when I began to research this action that Captain Albracht had not been present and the award had not been presented."

There was a reason for the omission: Albracht was late for the ceremony. He was busy trying to save another soldier's life.

Wind Is No Problem for a Lieutenant General

When Albracht woke up on Monday, November 3, 1969, a public information officer (PIO) from 5th Special Forces Group Headquarters in Nah Trang greeted him. The officer told the captain that there was a horde of media waiting to interview him about Kate. Albracht was not in the mood for an interview, but the officer assured him that the 5th Group commander, Col. "Iron Mike" Healey, insisted on it. It was another classic case of "duty calls."

The PIO rep went over a list of do's and don't's for Albracht to remember when speaking about the army's "gallant Vietnamese allies." Albracht wondered to himself to which "gallant Vietnamese allies" he was referring. He left the question unasked. So he showered, shaved, put on clean jungle fatigues, and faced the media circus that had gathered. He got through the press conference all right, but it was just a blur at the time.

Two days later, Albracht received a priority message from Lieutenant General Cochran ordering him to a ceremony at Ban Me Thuot to recognize the American defenders of Kate. He was even sending a special helicopter to pick up the captain. That promised to be an exciting event for anyone who would be on that chopper. The winds that day were blowing like Albracht had never seen before, and all "birds" were grounded—except for the slick that came for him. Apparently, Albracht, thought, "A lieutenant general outranks nature."

Not surprisingly, the chopper was late because of the weather. As it was on final approach, a Mike Force commander who had several seriously wounded Yards from the Buprang firefight approached Albracht. He had a problem: there were no other choppers available for medevac except the one Cochran had dispatched.

The commander asked Albracht if he would transport his wounded back to a field hospital in the Ban Me Thuot area, since the severity of their wounds precluded treatment at Buprang. It was truly a life-and-death situation. Albracht did not hesitate to make a decision.

He asked the pilot if he could perform a medevac first and then fly to the meeting with the general. The pilot allowed that he was told that this was Albracht's chopper. As far as he was concerned, he'd fly the captain wherever he wanted to go. The wounded troopers were loaded on the chopper and they departed for the field hospital.

At the hospital, Albracht assisted in getting the Yards to the emergency room and the chopper took off again for the general's ceremony. But time waits for no man, and neither do lieutenant generals.

Once the chopper landed, Albracht headed for the building to which he had been ordered to report. Instead of General Cochran, there was only general confusion. Lieutenant Mike Smith and several of the other troops from Kate greeted Albracht. Smith had a Silver Star pinned on his shirt.

Smith asked Albracht, "Where the hell were you?"

Albracht said simply, "I was unavoidably delayed."

Smith informed him that the general had waited a while, became irritated because Albracht was late, conducted the awards ceremony without him, and left, taking Albracht's medal with him. That caught the captain by surprise. It was the first he knew that it was to be an awards ceremony. The troops present told Albracht that he was supposed to receive a Silver Star as an "impact award." Albracht learned that the medal was to be upgraded once statements could be secured from the witnesses involved.

To Albracht, missing the awards ceremony was of little consequence compared to the actual events that had transpired over those six brutal days of escape and evasion. As he noted, "The lessons we learned about ourselves, the experiences we shared together, and the incredible bond that was forged in the heat of battle will live within us until our last breath."

Besides, he knew it would not do any good to hold his breath until he received a medal. What mattered to him was that he was back in the rear with the guys with whom he had shared so much. "We all felt we were due an in-country R&R, which is exactly what we did," he noted.

Oh Well, There Is Always Another Silver Star

There was some speculation among the troops that General Cochran had taken his medal and gone home because Albracht had snubbed him. Eventually, the explanation for the medal mix-up was determined. Special Forces was under the impression that the artillery command would write a recommendation for a decoration. The artillery command was under the impression that the Special Forces command would write it, since Albracht missed the award ceremony.

Brockwell believed firmly that Albracht deserved an award, as did the troops in his command who had been part of the E&E operation. He said, "The debriefing that I attended for the various groups of artillerymen from 5/27 and 5/22 artillery all left me with the belief that Captain Albracht's action had saved the lives of the twenty-one artillerymen left at Kate until the end. I can assure you that those men felt that way and that they felt a Silver Star was a minimal award."

When the dust settled, the paperwork was lost. Ironically, Albracht received the Silver Star in February 1970 for his heroism during the Buprang action on November 2, rather than for his exploits at Kate. That was small compensation for the lack of an award for his leadership leading up to and during the E&E, however.

Chapter 23

Once upon a Time

"A thing is not necessarily true because a man dies for it. Men die for what they want to be true, for what some terror in their hearts tells them is not true."

—OSCAR WILDE

There are three sides to every story: the right one, the wrong one, and the "in between." The third side is where the real story lies. Therefore, it makes sense to start with the North Vietnamese side of Kate. Their version begins with October 29, 1969, and tells a glowing story of how they annihilated the "puppet forces" at Kate (which the NVA called Ka Te):

> After a period of mobilizing all of our forces to carry out transport work on a line more than 70 km long, under torrential rain and B-52 carpet bombing, on the morning of 29 October, we began to attack and seize the Ka Te Base, thereby kicking off a new offensive along the entire enemy defense line from Buprang to Duclap.
>
> Ka Te was a mixed infantry-artillery base strongly built by the enemy on Peak 936, east of Buprang and 42 km northwest of Gia Nghia City. It was an important position in the

enemy's integrated firebase defense system. Stretching along the Vietnamese-Cambodian border, this system was designed to obstruct our attacks.

This base had nearly 100 Americans and 12 artillery pieces of various calibers. Here, the enemy had built 82 bunkers, barracks, supply depots, and a command post, half-buried underground. In the bases, the combat trenches were interconnected; surrounding the base was a dense barbed wire system rigged with several types of self-activated mines. Three puppet commando companies were responsible for perimeter defense. Every day, these puppets often pushed out far from the base to detect and prevent our attacks.

Early on 29 October, our artillery bombarded Ka Te, hitting and destroying the command post, artillery positions and bunkers, and annihilating infantry. At the same time, we used 82mm mortars in prearranged positions to keep in check enemy artillery positions in the surrounding hills, preventing them from aiding their comrades at Ka Te.

Meanwhile, our combat trenches kept pushing deeper into the enemy fences, tightly encircling the base. Seized by panic, the Americans called for help. Many of them who tried to flee by running out of the base were killed by mines, their bodies lying across the fences. A commando company conducting a search outside the base rushed back in panic, but was beaten to shreds. The enemy launched 186 sorties of various types of aircraft, strafing close to the fences in a bid to push us away and save their comrades, who were near death. But the combatants of the 66th Regiment kept tightening the noose day and night. Our AA machine gun units valiantly fought in open terrain, blowing up many U.S. planes, some of which burst into flames next to the fences, scaring the daylights out of the enemy inside.

Attacked day and night on the ground and in the air, the enemy became completely isolated. Their dead unburied, their wounded not evacuated for treatment, the living huddled in dark underground shelters filled with the stench of death. Anyone exposing himself above ground was immediately killed by our sniper fire. The enemy at Ka Te lacked food and water, their energy waned, their nerves were shot, their situation desperate. They begged for night airborne resupply, but all the air-dropped supplies fell into our hands. Combatants of the 49th Company, 40th Regiment, shot down U.S. aircraft in the middle of the night.

Faced with annihilation, an element of the enemy took advantage of darkness to flee the post on the sly, but its formation was directly fired on by our 12.7mm machine-gun crews. Many were killed, their bodies lying one on top of the other. The rest had to hurriedly retreat into the base. Not allowing the enemy to flee, at 0400 on 2 November, from encircling combat trenches, our infantry split into several spearheads and charged simultaneously, seizing control of the Ka Te Base.

Thus, after four days and nights of continually encircling and attacking, we had advanced and ended the battle, annihilating and seizing control of the Ka Te mixed infantry-artillery base, wiping out nearly 200, including 70 Americans, shooting down 14 aircraft, and seizing six 105mm Howitzers and dozens of tons of ammunition.

This was a successful attack of the theater against a fortified position; it had great tactical value. With our lack of self-propelled artillery and tanks to completely overwhelm the enemy and quickly decide the battle, our troops had upheld their sense of ceaselessly attacking. Unable to conclude their assault by night, they stuck to their position and continued to attack by day; unable to complete their attack in one day, they struck for several days until the position was overwhelmed. The infantry had extended its combat trenches deep into enemy fences and tightly encircled their troops, thereby preventing them from fleeing and limited our casualties from aircraft and artillery.

Our artillery knew how to use to maximum effectiveness various kinds of portable artillery to keep enemy artillery positions and airfields in check while annihilating targets inside the base with direct fire, which helped our infantry. Various kinds of AA guns were moved close to the enemy's fences to simultaneously wipe them out inside the post and prevent aircraft from bombing to close breaches and strike at our combat trenches. With that creative and no-holds-barred fighting method, we besieged them, gradually wearing down and weakening them, then completely defeating them.

This method strengthened our troops' confidence and created proper conditions for attacking fortified positions—a new requirement posed for the theater in the development of the war of liberation. After razing Ka Te, our infantry, artillery, and elite forces repeatedly struck at a string of remaining positions from Buprang to Duclap.

At the same time, they fiercely intercepted and attacked enemy relief columns. Acting in close coordination with the main direction, we also unleashed repeated attacks in Gia Nghia, Kien Duc, Nhan Co, and Ban Me Thuot, 113 miles northeast of Saigon.

After more than one month of extremely valiant and fierce fighting (29 October–5 December), we had knocked out of action the 220th and 53d Battle Groups and one mixed battle group and seized or destroyed positions on the Buprang-Duclap defense line, thereby upsetting their disposition in the south Dac Lac-Quang Duc theater.[*]

The *History of the 66th Regiment—the Plei Me Group—1947–2007* tells just as heroic a story. The report suggests that the regiment wiped out the force at Kate, long after they had left the building.

---

[*] *People's Armed Forces of the Central Highlands During the Resistance War against the Americans to Save the Nation* (Hanoi: People's Army Publishing House, 1980), 186–90.

In late October 1969, the 66th Regiment, the 28th Regiment, and several artillery units launched a wave of attacks against the enemy's Buprang-Duclap defense line.

During the early morning hours of 29 October, the regiment's 8th Battalion and 1st Company/7th Battalion opened fire to launch the attack and siege of the enemy's Ka Te Base. Two 75mm recoilless rifles of the 15th Company, deployed 600 meters from the enemy base, knocked out enemy bunkers and gun positions on the outer perimeter. At the same time the division ordered its 82mm mortars to place suppressive fire on the enemy artillery position on hilltops in the surrounding area to prevent them from providing fire support to their fellow soldiers at Ka Te.

Utilizing the cover of our artillery bombardment, our infantrymen pushed fighting trenches deep into the enemy's barbed wire perimeter fence and tightened their siege ring around the enemy. The soldiers inside the base were terrified and screamed to be rescued. Many of the enemy soldiers tried to flee but stepped on mines. Their dead bodies lay draped over the perimeter wire.

The enemy sent in a total of 187 air sorties, including both jets and helicopter gunships, that bombed and strafed the area right along the perimeter wire to try to push our forces back away from the base. Our 12.7mm machine gunners who were accompanying our infantrymen heroically fought back and shot down many enemy aircraft. One enemy aircraft burst into flames and crashed right next to the base, terrifying the defenders even more.

After three days of being surrounded and under siege, the defenders were out of drinking water and food and were begging to be rescued. C-130s dropped supplies, but almost all of the supply pallets dropped by the aircraft ended up in the hands of our troops.

At 4:00 in the morning of 2 November, the opportunity to overrun the Ka Te Base had arrived. Regiment Commander

Ho De ordered the regiment's 8th Battalion to attack. After one hour of fighting, 8th Battalion and 1st Company/7th Battalion had seized control of the entire base, killed almost 200 enemy soldiers (including 70 Americans), captured 8 prisoners, shot down 14 aircraft, and captured two intact 155mm Howitzers and six 105mm Howitzers as well as thousands of artillery shells and all of the base's supplies.

The 66th Regiment's attack that overran and destroyed the composite infantry-artillery battalion defending Ka Te was of tremendous value from the tactical standpoint. During this battle our soldiers had demonstrated their high resolve to attack the enemy, fighting day and night, and when the battle was not over at the end of the first day, they continued to fight, day after day, until the objective was finally taken.

During the course of the fighting the regiment had used only its own organic heavy weapons to conduct the attack on Ka Te, and this built confidence in our troops and set a precedent for future attacks against enemy troops holding solid fortified positions, thereby meeting a new requirement that had been set for the troops of the Central Highlands.

During this same period, 2nd Company/7th Battalion, led by Company Commander Nguyen Dinh Kiep, conducted a continuous, day-long assault on Hill 882 that killed almost 200 enemy troops and captured 120 individual enemy fortifications.

In the end, the puppet 5th CIDG Battalion holding this position was forced to retreat. By advancing, digging in, and then attacking again, and keeping this up until the enemy position was completely overrun, 2nd Battalion had crippled a puppet army battalion that had occupied a dug-in field defensive position.

After overrunning the enemy's Ka Te Base, the infantrymen and artillerymen of the 66th Regiment launched a wave of attacks against the remaining enemy positions in the Buprang area. At the same time, our troops also blocked and attacked enemy relief columns that had arrived to try to clear the area, eliminating from the field of battle the enemy's 220th Task Force and another regimental-sized task force.

On 5 December 1969, the southern Central Highlands operation came to an end.

As soon as the sounds of gunfire had ended, the 66th Regiment held a ceremony to inform the late Uncle Ho of its successes. Every man felt happy as the unit offered to the spirit of Uncle Ho the unit's outstanding achievement, which was that for the first time the regiment had annihilated an entire composite infantry-artillery battalion occupying a solidly fortified position.

During this campaign our forces had achieved a high level of combat efficiency by killing large numbers of enemy troops while keeping our own casualties low. The day after the ceremony, the regiment and the other friendly units that had participated in this wave of operations marched out to return to the northern sector as quickly as possible.[*]

The "puppet" (i.e., friendly) survivors of the siege of LZ Kate and the battle for Buprang and Duclap tell a different story. Participants on both sides agree that there was a battle in that part of Vietnam in the last quarter of 1969. They don't agree on much else about the strategies employed, the numbers of casualties and numbers of aircraft shot down, the escape of any "puppets" from Kate, or the ultimate outcome. No doubt the truth lies somewhere in between.

---

[*] *History of the 66th Regiment—the Plei Me Group—1947–2007* (Hanoi: People's Army Publishing House, 2007).

Chapter 24

All for Naught?

"The Wall in Washington is missing about a million names . . . the
casualties of the war that no one ever really bothered to count . . .
the names of the families and loved ones whose lives were changed
when one of those names on the wall was taken from them."

—PAT EWING, BLUE STAR 114 (1969–70)

The siege had ended, and the troops returned to relative safety at Buprang and survived an attack almost immediately afterwards. The NVA simply would not give up. It made one final attempt to capture Buprang, which kept the friendly forces on their toes. The friendly forces not only expected new attacks on the base, but they were well prepared for them.

For some reason, the NVA did not attack in force immediately. Skirmishes around Buprang continued. Lattin in particular remained active. He and Albracht reconnected once again—once again under stressful circumstances.

Lattin II

Lattin, who likened flying a plane without a propeller to driving a train without a smokestack, was flying a mission on November 13 when he spotted Vietnam Air Force (VNAF) A-37 jets in the middle of an attack on ground troops. Something did not look right to Lattin. He had a keen eye.

Lattin's initial assessment of the attack was correct: the A-37 pilots were bombing their own troops, killing twenty-three of them. He flew his plane directly into the path of the jets in an effort to alert them to their error. The VNAF pilots got the hint and broke off the attack, which saved more ARVN troops from death or injury. That ended his day, but Lattin's adventures involving Albracht continued. Three days later he flew into harm's way again, with disastrous results.

Buprang came under heavy fire from the Cambodian side of the border on November 16. Lattin was flying as FAC in his O-1 Birddog that day, directing U.S. Air Force air strikes on targets that were just over the border in Cambodia. Lattin flew toward the target to mark it for a flight of F-100s, Dusty 61 and Dusty 62, when his plane took a serious hit.

"As I rolled in, I put in three marks; the first one on two guns and then kicked rudder to the right and marked a location with two smokes that had four guns," he explained. "I got hit right front, took out the right side of the cockpit, along with all radios except FM along with elevator and ailerons, then exited through the top."

Lattin got on the radio and contacted Buprang. Albracht answered his call.

"Hawk, I'm going down," Lattin announced.

Albracht responded in his usual calm voice.

"Don't worry," he said. "We're coming to get you, even if we have to send out a whole regiment."

Of course, Albracht didn't have a regiment at his disposal, but that was not a problem. As it turned out, Lattin managed to land his plane at Buprang, but it was not an easy task. He steered his plane in through heavy artillery and mortar fire blanketing the dirt landing strip at the base. As he approached, a heavy crosswind sprang up and buffeted the base. Albracht talked him down as a bevy of soldiers worked furiously to remove a wire-and-wood barrier that impeded his approach.

Miraculously, Lattin avoided the barrier and flew in between the artillery and mortar shells pouring down on the base. He landed safely and relatively unscathed. Lattin and his copilot, 2nd Lt. Walter C. Phillips, incurred some minor scratches on their faces. Undaunted, they were both back in the air quickly, where their services were needed badly.

U.S. bombers launched an attack on suspected NVA troop concentrations right after Lattin landed. They were located somewhere along the Vietnam-Cambodia border in relatively unpopulated areas, perhaps around Camp Le Rolland, where Albracht had long suspected NVA troops had a base.

The pilots could not be sure if the targets they hit were in Cambodia or Vietnam. The distinction was unclear. The region was not clearly mapped, and the people living in it had fled long ago to refugee centers. The pilots reported that they saw two large secondary explosions after they made their runs. Whatever they hit it did not dissuade the NVA from continuing its attacks.

Air Power Continues to Make the Difference

The NVA continued to attack Buprang and Duclap, twenty-five miles north, from inside Cambodia. They had forced the closures of Kate, Susan, and Annie, but the two Special Forces camps, defended mostly by Montagnards and Cambodian mercenaries, were different stories. They were better defended and afforded aircraft more maneuverability. Neither factor stopped the NVA attacks.

On November 17, South Vietnamese and NVA troops engaged in a four-hour battle less than two miles from Buprang. According to South Vietnamese reports, casualties included sixteen NVA troops killed, compared to two friendly soldiers killed and five wounded.

The fighting continued for the next couple days. On November 18, NVA troops, repeating the same tactics used against Kate, attacked Buprang at dawn, simultaneously firing mortars from nearby and artillery from Cambodia. That brought an immediate—and potentially disastrous—retaliation.

U.S. fighter-bomber jets carried out blistering attacks along a ridgeline just a little east of the base, where approximately 800 North

Vietnamese troops were lying in wait according to South Vietnamese estimates. Allegedly, the combination of U.S. and South Vietnamese air and ground attacks killed 243 NVA troops, although the number may have been exaggerated—a common practice by both sides during the war.

At any rate, the fighting in the area continued unabated through the rest of 1969 and into 1970. There was no clear-cut winner. About the only conclusions historians reached after the war was that the battles for the Special Forces camps at Benhet, Dak To, Buprang, and Duc Lap had been major tests of Nixon's Vietnamization policy, and there was no evidence it had been successful.

The friendly forces could claim victory at Benhet and Buprang–Duclap, but not because the ARVN had performed well enough to defeat the NVA decisively. The difference was air power, most of it provided by U.S. forces.

General Abrams told Secretary of Defense Melvin Laird in early 1970 that the ARVN's big battles of the previous year had been in the Central Highlands. He cited four in particular, all fights for Special Forces camps. Joint Chiefs of Staff historians writing after American forces had left the war agreed that Benhet had been the key engagement of 1969. The ARVN largely failed in the Highlands campaign. Benhet stood under siege for weeks without the South Vietnamese sector commander at Dak To breaking up the concentration, which allowed the enemy to reach past Benhet to strike at Dak To itself.

The NVA troops failed to capture either place, despite using tanks against Benhet. But the defenders there were mostly CIDG strikers, Special Forces, Nungs (an ethnic group that supplied mercenaries to Mike Force and other friendly units), and American artillerymen, with a lesser contingent of South Vietnamese. It took the ARVN four months to disengage the camp.

Secret American reports on ARVN performance show the desertion rate for the main unit in this sector, the 42nd Infantry, ran 20 percent higher than for the ARVN as a whole. Benhet was won by air power, not ground troops. The Americans had furnished all the Arc Lights and nine-tenths of the tactical air support.

Buprang came under siege during the last months of 1969, and the battle spilled over to Duclap. The campaign featured the loss of several nearby firebases. MACV said it deliberately withheld help other than air power in order to test Vietnamization. But the aircraft saved the day here, too. When a rescue force of the 23rd ARVN Division finally arrived at Duclap, its regimental commander denounced the leader of the defending ARVN regiment as a coward and expelled him and his troops from the camp.

The arguments about who won the battles and whether Vietnamization was successful were transparent to the artillerymen and Special Forces troops who had barely escaped Benhet, Dak To, and the firebases around Buprang and Duclap with their lives. That was especially true of the defenders of Kate, most of whom had survived one of the most harrowing E&Es of the Vietnam War, thanks to the leadership of Dan Pierelli and William Albracht.

Lessons Learned

After the battle for Duclap and Buprang ended, the search for information about the outcome, termed "Lessons Learned" by the army, began. The analysis often involves a good deal of finger-pointing and scapegoating, especially when a battle or campaign does not turn out well.

Reasons explaining the exodus from Kate varied. Some critics suggested that the South Vietnamese command did not want to risk the limited number of troops available for rescue work lest a more demanding situation develop elsewhere. Others tied it to Nixon's Vietnamization policy.

Reginald Brockwell suggested that it might have been a combination of factors. Brockwell drew a parallel between the May 1969 siege of Benhet and the attacks on Duclap and Buprang. He explained that "The ARVN 24th STZ and ARVN 23rd Division showed a hesitancy to become involved to support or reinforce the action. They felt that no more resources should be expended." Likewise, he noted, "Since this was a test of Vietnamization, the U.S. command would not commit American ground troops. Politics, not firepower, doomed these isolated firebases."

Brockwell averred that when planning started for Kate, Susan, Annie, and so on, some of the people who had participated in the Benhet siege felt that, as then, these three firebases were being used as bait to draw a large force of NVA into the target zone of U.S. airpower. If that was the case, it worked.

According to Brockwell, the fact that South Vietnamese Marine Col. Nguyen Ba Lien was commanding the ARVN 24th STZ at Benhet reinforced this theory. When he had been involved with the fifty-five-day siege of Benhet earlier in 1969, he stated in an interview picked up by *Stars and Stripes* and the *New York Times* that he had always intended to use lightly defended Benhet as "bait" to lure the NVA across the border where they would be engaged by American artillery and air power.

In December 1969, Colonel Lien was killed when his helicopter was shot down. *Stars and Stripes* ran headlines that said "Vietnamization working at Buprang" and "ARVN Are Clobbering Charlie." The text in one article said that the ARVN was doing most of the major fighting while the Montagnard forces had experienced little contact. Those who were involved knew the real story. In fact, Brockwell stressed, "These actions and the failure of the Vietnamization process came to the attention of General Creighton Abrams who, by my reading, blamed the Special Forces unjustly for these failures." But arguing the true causes was a bit like the chicken-versus-the-egg debate: nobody knew for sure, but the discussion went on.

As Tevye Says . . .

Inevitably, the troops and the brass made different assessments of the events. Both groups have myopic views of a battle or campaign. The troops who do the actual fighting are somewhat limited in their opinions, since they see a very small portion of the battlefield and have a mutual distrust for the high-ranking officers who do the planning and make the decisions. As Tevye was fond of saying in *The Fiddler on the Roof,* "On the other hand . . ."

The high-ranking officers often view battles and campaigns from afar. They have a bird's-eye view of what goes on, making decisions on the fly as action reports come into their HQs behind the lines. They may have a better overview of the whole battlefield, but their ability to see the individual actions on it are restricted. Thus, they have to wait until a battle or campaign ends to analyze what happened.

The brass sifts through after-action reports provided by participants in the battle or campaign, interviews with officers and enlisted personnel, recordings of conversations between and among personnel, and other sources as they compile their "Lessons Learned" histories. Those histories may be classified and hidden for years until some government bureaucrats decide it is safe to release them for public consumption. The documents may or may not be redacted and edited, depending on their importance and sensitivity. In any case, they rarely contain the complete story about an event, battle, campaign, etc. After all, they are produced by humans who may want to protect the reputations of certain people involved in events, safeguard national security, eliminate the possibility of offending allies . . . the list goes on.

For whatever reason, the lessons learned about the siege of Kate and its sister bases and the entire battle for control of the Central Highlands region of Vietnam may never reflect accurately what really happened between September 1, 1969, and December 31, 1969. That does not stop people from theorizing about the real causes that led up to the E&E of Kate and the other firebases and the enemy attacks on Buprang and Duclap. As far as the defenders of Kate were concerned, they were just pleased to be alive and able to report to their next duty assignments.

Out of the Dairy Queen and into Mike Force

It was time for a new assignment for Albracht. The question was where. Colonel "Iron Mike" Healey, who served five and a half tours in Vietnam, leading the 5th Special Forces group for almost twenty months, flew to Buprang very soon after Kate and told Albracht how proud he was of him. Albracht's team was in formation watching and listening to the presentation. Albracht was a little embarrassed.

Healey asked Albracht where he wanted to go, even offering him a position as his aide. Jokingly, Albracht asked to be assigned as the officer in charge of the Na Tranh Dairy Queen (there actually was an ice cream joint at HQ). Although his men got a great kick out of the request, Iron Mike was less than amused.

Healey looked at Albracht and, in a not-too-friendly manner, told him that the position was filled already. Albracht had an alternative available.

"How about the Mike Force?" he asked.

"You got it," Healey replied.

Then the colonel did an abrupt about-face, got on the chopper, and left. Albracht became a member of Mike Force, the same unit whose members had risked their lives to link up with him and his E&E group after their harrowing escape from Kate.

Epilogue

Where Are They Now

John F. Ahearn (WO-1). John Ahearn graduated from flight school at Fort Rucker in Class 68-43 and arrived in Vietnam early in 1969, where he was assigned immediately to the 155th Assault Helicopter Company, a unit of the 10th Combat Aviation Battalion, in Ban Me Thuot. He continued to fly with the 155th until December 4, 1969, when he was wounded in the legs carrying out a medevac mission on the "Volcano" in nearby Duc Lap. Ahearn was evacuated out of Vietnam on December 8 (his birthday) and spent a number of months hospitalized back in the U.S. He was promoted to CW-2 and in the fall of 1970 was retired on disability as the result of his wounds. He returned to school and completed an undergraduate degree in accounting and an MBA in finance. He enjoyed a long career as a CPA and business executive in the New York City area, where he and his wife, Natalie, raised their two sons. In 1999, they relocated to Scottsdale, Arizona, where they continue to reside.

William L. "Bill" Albracht (ground commander at Kate). Born and raised in Rock Island, Illinois, Albracht graduated from Alleman High School in 1966 and joined the U.S. Army. He attended Infantry Officer Candidate School and was commissioned a second lieutenant in 1967 at the age of nineteen. He spent his commissioned career in the U.S. Army Special Forces, commonly referred to as the "Green Berets." At age twenty-one, Bill was the youngest captain to command combat troops during the Vietnam War. As the recipient of two Silver Stars for gallantry in action, three Purple Hearts, five Bronze Stars, as well as other awards for combat valor, Bill is one of the most highly decorated veterans in the state of Illinois.

Upon his discharge from the military, he worked his way through college, graduating with an associate's degree from Black Hawk College and a bachelor's degree from Augustana College. After graduation, he became a special agent in the U.S. Secret Service, protecting our nation's leaders (including several presidents), their families, and visiting foreign dignitaries for more than twenty-five years. He was also featured on the Discovery Channel's *Secrets of the Secret Service* program.

In 1989, Bill returned to the Quad Cities area with his three children, whom he raised as a single parent, while working as a resident agent for the Secret Service. After retiring in early 2001, Bill went to the Ford Motor Company as the manager of Ford's Executive Security Operations. After once again feeling the pull of home, Bill moved back to the Quad Cities in 2005. Bill currently lives in Moline, Illinois, and works as an independent security consultant. Bill is married to the lovely and talented Mary Moran of Coal Valley, and together they have five children and seven grandchildren.

Reginald Brockwell (architect of Firebase Kate). His first child, a daughter, was born shortly after Kate, in December 1969. Brockwell spent the rest of his tour with A Battery, 5/22 Artillery. In March 1970, he returned to Fort Sill, Oklahoma, to complete his active-duty military obligation as an assistant S-3 with 8/17 Artillery. Then he returned to Shell Oil in Houston, where he had been a chemical engineer prior to his military service. Shell laid him off after a year. In December 1971, he entered the financial services field as a stock and commodities broker. Eventually, he became a registered investment advisor. He retired in July 2006. Since then, he has spent his time volunteering for several nonprofits serving the disadvantaged. He lives in Houston with his wife, whom he married in August 1968. He has two daughters.

Ken Donovan (last supply pilot into Kate). After the resupply mission into LZ Kate, CW2 Donovan continued to fly combat missions during the battle of Buprang–Duclap for another six weeks, until his combat tour ended on December 5, 1969. Upon his return to the United States, he was assigned as an instructor pilot at the U.S. Army's Primary Helicopter Training School at Fort Wolters, Texas, until his release from active duty in January 1971. Donovan joined the

Michigan Army National Guard in 1971, accepting a direct commission to second lieutenant. He ended his twenty-eight-year military career in 1995 after rising to the rank of lieutenant colonel. During his subsequent civilian career, Donovan held a number of defense industry positions, finally retiring in 2009 as vice president of sales and marketing for AOM Engineering. Now fully retired, he lives with his wife, Cheryl, in Brooksville, Florida.

Al Dykes. He flew the last Spooky gunship mission in Vietnam, on November 30, 1969. Everybody in the squadron and three FOs were reassigned, except for him and one enlisted man. They had the sad job of closing down the Spooky Mission in Vietnam. This took the entire month of December 1969. On Dykes's return to the U.S. in January 1970, he was assigned to Dyess Air Force Base, Abilene, Texas, flying a C-130. After five years at Dyess, he was assigned to the MC-130E Combat Talon Mission and spent two and a half years in Okinawa, Japan. He returned to Hurlburt Field, Fort Walton Beach, Florida, in 1978, still flying the MC-130E. He retired in 1984 and opened a clock shop in Fort Walton Beach. In 1989, Dykes was hired to develop a training program for the new MC-130 Combat Talon II aircraft for the U.S. Air Force. He spent all of the 1990s setting up the Talon II program and simulator and training air crews in Albuquerque, New Mexico. He returned to Fort Walton Beach in 2001, where he continued his clock-repair work, all the while trying to determine why he can't do many of things he could do forty years ago. His wife said it was because he's seventy-four years old, but he didn't believe her.

Harold ("Ben") Gay (Joker 73, 48th Assault Helicopter Company). Gay joined the U.S. Army in 1967. He served two tours in Vietnam, first with the 155th AHC (1968–69) and then with the 48th AHC (1969–70) He was discharged from the active army at Fort Eustis, Virginia, in November 1971. Within a week he joined the Virginia Army National Guard as a gunship pilot in an assault helicopter company as part of the 28th Infantry Division. The AHC gunship platoon was changed to the 986th Helicopter Medevac detachment in 1980. The unit was activated and sent to Fort Bragg, North Carolina, for Desert Shield in September 1990, and was then deployed to Saudi

Arabia in January 1991 as part of Desert Storm, where it served with the 7th Corps. The unit flew combat medevac missions in support of allied forces in Saudi Arabia, Kuwait, and Iraq until June 1991, including medevacs of wounded U.S. Marines from Kuwait International Airport as they fought to retake it in February 1991. Gay retired from the Virginia Army National Guard and the U.S. military in September 1995, with twenty-eight years of service, including over 4,000 hours of flight time, almost 1,500 hours of which were combat time. He began his college career in January 1972 and received his bachelor's degree from Christopher Newport College of the College of William and Mary in December 1974. He was then employed by the U.S. government as a special agent with the Naval Criminal Investigative Service (NCIS) and then as a special agent with the U.S. Treasury Department for the next twenty-five years. His career as a law enforcement/special agent, which coincided with his National Guard career, included investigating criminal activity, undercover assignments, protection of presidents and presidential candidates, and various assignments in eastern Europe after the collapse of the USSR. Gay retired from the U.S. government in July 2000. One week later, he began his third career as a patrol deputy sheriff with the New Kent Sheriff's Office in Virginia. As of September 2012, he was still a patrol deputy and also responsible for marine patrol. He and his wife, Janet, have been blessed with twenty-four years of marriage, a son, daughter-in-law, and two wonderful grandchildren.

Anthony ("Tony") Giordano. He was in Army ROTC at CCNY in New York and was commissioned a second lieutenant in January 1967 in the Corps of Engineers. He graduated with a bachelor of architecture degree. In March 1967, he went to the Corps of Engineers Officer Training School at Fort Belvoir, Virginia. In September 1967, he attended helicopter flight school at Fort Wolters, Texas, and Hunter Army Airfield, Georgia. After getting his wings in May 1968, he was assigned as a helicopter pilot in the 2nd Armored Division at Fort Hood, Texas. He received his Vietnam orders in December 1968, arriving in January 1969 as a first lieutenant assigned to the 155th AHC. After a couple of months as a platoon leader and assistant operations officer, he made captain in March 1969. Soon thereafter, he was appointed as the 155th operations officer, in which capacity he served from about May through December 1969. He returned to the U.S. at the end of December 1969, where he was separated immediately from the army because his three-year commitment had been satisfied. As a civilian, he returned to New York with his wife and daughter.

Kenn Hopkins handled the 155 projectiles. After he left Kate, Hopkins was assigned to LZ Mike Smith, where the troops received almost daily rocket fire but no ground attacks. After LZ Smith, he was given charge of a gun section, even though he was an E-4 holding down a E-6 position. The assignment was in recognition of his actions on Kate. The last firebase on which he served was Suzie, outside of An Khe. Two days after he left Suzie, he was in Washington to get his discharge from the army. Hopkins got out of the army after serving only one and a half years because he was drafted and left Vietnam with six months left to serve. Like many Vietnam veterans, he could not relate to anyone when he got home, so he "ran away" to Europe for four months to "come down" from the experience. After returning to the United States, Hopkins became a math major at San Diego State University. He then became a gardener for fifteen years, after which he started working for Great American Bank in San Diego. He worked his way up to become vice president of its subsidiary, California General Mortgage Service. After the bank was taken over by the RTC, he worked for Chicago Title Company and returned to school to earn a degree in computer programming. He currently works for a company that provides computer applications for a "special client." Hopkins lives in Chula Vista, California, and surfs every weekend he can.

Bob Johnson departed Vietnam on December 25, 1969, for Fort Lewis in Washington. Later that day, he received his honorable discharge from the army and returned to his home in Rhode Island, arriving there on December 26. Three days later, he reported back to his pre-army job as an actuarial associate at The Equitable Life Assurance Society in New York City. Johnson, who had become an associate of the Society of Actuaries during 1968, passed his final examinations to become a fellow during 1972. He retired in 1993. Johnson married Carol Cravens, of Quincy, Illinois, in 1971, following her graduation from Knox College. The couple raised three boys in Westport, Connecticut, where two became Eagle Scouts and the other a Life Scout. Johnson served for several years as the chairman of the troop committee. He and Carol moved to North Myrtle Beach, South Carolina, where they are enjoying retirement.

John Kerr (FDC officer at Kate). After being treated for thirty days in Pleiku and Cam Ranh Bay hospitals for wounds sustained at Kate, Kerr spent time at many other firebases for nine months, often with Lt. Mike Smith. In 1970, after he returned from Vietnam, he was promoted to captain and taught gunnery and ballistics at the U.S. Army Field Artillery School at Fort Sill, Oklahoma. He left the army in 1971, after which he held a variety of engineering positions at Alliant Energy's nuclear power plant in Cedar Rapids, Iowa. He retired in 2001. Since then, he has been a part-time math teacher at Kirkwood College in Cedar Rapids.

Nelson Koon. After Kate, Koon still had about eleven months left on his tour in Vietnam. He spent them at many more landing zones and firebases—none as intense as Kate.

Koon left Vietnam in October 1970 and served as a drill sergeant until his discharge in August 1972. After that, he worked various jobs, such as tree trimmer, foundry worker, and laborer. Koon served with the Washington Army National Guard from 1977 through 1989. He was a full-time active-duty career counselor for three of those years. He lived in Tacoma, Washington, from 1972 through 1982. He was married in 1974, and his only daughter was born in 1976. He has since divorced and remarried. Koon resided in Vancouver, Washington, from 1982 until 2002 and in New Mexico from 2002 to 2012. He received an associate's degree in 1983 and was awarded 100 percent VA disability and Social Security in 2006 for PTSD, Agent Orange exposure, hearing loss, and various other medical problems.

George Robert Lattin (WALT 20). Lattin, a retired U.S. Air Force pilot, passed away October 22, 2006, at the age of seventy-five. He had been a resident of Fort Worth, Texas, for more than thirty years. Lattin had retired from the air force in 1970 as a major with twenty-two years of service and 10,000 flying hours as a pilot. His military awards include the Silver Star, two Distinguished Flying Crosses, the Bronze Star, the Purple Heart, twelve Air Medals, three Commendation Medals, and many other service ribbons and awards. After his retirement, he was a salesman and sales manager for Pitney Bowes, from which he retired in 1989.

Dean Owen was the commanding officer of the 155th AHC and flight leader during the night resupply mission into LZ Kate. Following his assignment with the 155th, he returned to the States and continued to serve in a variety of staff and command assignments. His last assignment was as the Aviation Brigade Commander, 6th Infantry Division, stationed at Fort Wainwright, Alaska. He retired on October 31, 1990, with the rank of colonel after thirty years of active duty with the U. S. Army. Following military service, he worked in rural airport management for the Alaska Department of Transportation and Public Facilities. He and his wife live in Fairbanks, Alaska.

Dan Pierelli. Originally from West Haven, Connecticut, Pierelli always felt he wanted to serve his country. He earned admission to the U.S. Air Force Academy and loved it there, but he left after one semester and entered the Air Force Reserves. He floundered for about a year and a half and decided to join the Air Force and go into pararescue. But the Air Force would not guarantee the assignment, and Pierelli got released from the reserves, joined the army, and entered Airborne/Special Forces. He served with the 6th Special Forces at Fort Bragg, the 5th Special Forces in Vietnam (March 1969–April 1970), and the 10th Special Forces at Fort Devens, Massachusetts (April–August 1970). After leaving the service in 1970, he returned to school and earned a bachelor of science and a couple master's degrees. Pierelli worked for two local defense firms while establishing his own lawn and painting business. Currently, he substitute teaches at middle and high schools, which he enjoys immensely. Pierelli married his wife, Maria, in 1971. They had met in 1967 before he left for basic. They have two sons, Carlo and Anthony. He and Maria travel around the U.S. as much as possible, visiting national parks and their sons.

Michael R. Norton. On May 1, 1978, Norton was officially declared a casualty of the Vietnam War. He is Panel 16W, Line 023 on the Vietnam Memorial in Washington, DC.

Gerald V. ("Tex") Rogers was discharged in 1970. He went on to have a family, became a professional steer wrestler in the Professional Rodeo Cowboys Association, and started his own construction company in Crane, Texas. After fighting a long battle with diabetes, he passed away in 1995.

Ronald A. Ross attended Muskego High School in Wisconsin and was a member of the varsity wrestling team. After high school, Ross attended the University of Wisconsin, majoring in marine biology. After a year and a half, he decided to put his education on hold and joined the U.S. Army. Ron left for basic training at Fort Leonard Wood, Missouri, on February 23, 1966. He earned the Outstanding Trainee Trophy at graduation, and was selected to attend Army Leadership School, where he chose the Field Artillery branch. He was commissioned a second lieutenant on December 15, 1967, at Fort Sill, Oklahoma, and wore his father's lieutenant bars in tribute. He was then assigned to Fort Irwin, California, and subsequently sent to Panama for final training before deploying to Vietnam in December 1968. Ross was initially assigned to Headquarters and Headquarters Battery, 5th Battalion, 22nd Artillery. He soon volunteered to take command of a 105 howitzer platoon after the officer in charge was wounded during the action. Ross reported to Firebase Kate, working for Capt. William L. Albracht.

Mike Smith. Ending his Vietnam service as executive officer of Charlie Battery in 1970, Smith was promoted to captain and assigned to command C Battery, 3/79th FA, Honest John Rocket, Giessen, West Germany, until 1973. He left military service in 1975, returned to Colorado and family life, raised two sons, attended college, and ultimately became a professor of veterinary anatomy and histology, teaching at Colorado State University, Ross University (St. Kitts), and St. George's University. For the last eighteen years, he and his wife, Beth, have lived aboard their sailboat *Justin's Odyssey*, currently anchored in Grenada.

Mike Wilcox. Wilcox returned to the States on Thanksgiving Day 1969, very shortly after the Buprang–LZ Kate siege. He was assigned duty at Fort Rucker, Alabama, where he worked on the ranges, training WOCs on armament systems. His term of service expired October 2,

1970. Mike and his wife, Shirley, returned to his hometown of Sacramento, California, where he attended college and worked in the oil refineries until 1976. For the next two years, he worked in a nuclear power plant as an operator. During this period, he started working in the home construction field. He ultimately left the nuclear plant job to pursue a career in home building. In 1978, feeling overwhelmed by the influx of people, rising property taxes, and the fast pace of living, Mike and his family left on a two-month road trip covering twenty-seven states. They liked the slower small-town pace of his wife's hometown of Brantley, Alabama, so much they moved back there. Shirley and Mike raised two sons who now live within two miles of them. Shirley is the town barber, and Mike had to retire from his construction business in 2009 due to prostate cancer. They have spent years and logged thousands upon thousands of miles on horseback and trail riding. They now spend most of their free time watching their two granddaughters play fast-pitch softball.

Acknolwedgments

This book would not have been possible without the contributions of soldiers, airmen, and civilians who wanted to make sure the story of Firebase Kate was told. Special thanks go to Ken Moffet, the coordinator of the story collection for this book and a military police veteran of Vietnam.